4b—

K

WEN BON

A NAVAL AIR INTELLIGENCE OFFICER

BEHIND JAPANESE LINES IN CHINA

WEN BON

A NAVAL AIR INTELLIGENCE OFFICER

BEHIND JAPANESE LINES IN CHINA

BYRON R. WINBORN

NUMBER 2 WAR AND THE SOUTHWEST SERIES

UNIVERSITY OF NORTH TEXAS PRESS

First printed in 1994 in the United States of America

10 9 8 7 6 5 4 3 2 1

The paper in this book meets the minimum requirements of the American
National Standard for Permanence of paper for Printed Library materials,
z39.48-1984.

Library of Congress Cataloging-in-Publication Data

Winborn, Byron R., 1910–
    Wen Bon : a Naval Air Intelligence Officer behind Japanese Lines in
China / by Byron R. Winborn.
        p. cm. — (War and the Southwest Series : no. 2)
    Includes index.
    ISBN 0-929398-77-7
    1. Sino-Japanese Conflicts, 1937–1945—Personal narratives, American. 2.
Winborn, Byron R., 1910–   . I. Title. II. Series.
DS777.5315W56 1994
952.03'3'092—dc20   94-17451
                                                               CIP

Cover design by Aaron Pendland

War and the Southwest Series

The University of North Texas Press has undertaken to publish a series of significant books about War and the Southwest. This broad category includes first-hand accounts of military experiences by men and women of the Southwest, histories of warfare involving the people of the Southwest, and analyses of military life in the Southwest itself. The Southwest is defined loosely as those states of the United States west of the Mississippi River and south of a line from San Francisco to St. Louis as well as the borderlands straddling the Mexico-United States boundary. The series will include works involving military life in peacetime in addition to books on warfare itself. It will range chronologically from the first contact between indigenous tribes and Europeans to the present. The series is based on the belief that warfare is an important if unfortunate fact of life in human history and that understanding war is a requirement for a full understanding of the American past.

General Series Editors

Richard G. Lowe
Gustav L. Seligmann
Calvin Christman

Other books in the Series

Foo—A Japanese-American Prisoner of the Rising Sun
An Artist at War: The Journal of John Gaitha Browning

DEDICATION

This series of sketches is dedicated to my beloved wife, Maggie, the one who persuaded me to write them up after all these years.

She did so even though the sketches tell about events that occurred a couple of years before the two of us even met. Moreover, she knew full well that the tedious task of typing the manuscript would devolve upon her.

TABLE OF CONTENTS

PREFACE

It is really inane for me to write about the experiences I had in China. All military men who were out there have better stories to tell than I. Stateside civilians simply cannot identify with the psychology and reactions involved. Those facing some of those wild situations were, or certainly should have been, psychologically reconstructed beings. This was accomplished through prolonged training, preparation, and contemplation. They became very different people than they had been a few months before, with different reactions to dangerous hardship and pitiable scenes.

When the adventure was all over, they would gradually revert to type—more or less. They never again became quite the bland civilians they had been before it all started.

One of the principal things we newcomers to China had to learn was how to pronounce the names of the provinces, cities and villages we were going to visit. We were instructed to give the letter "k" either a "j" sound or a "g" sound, "p" a "b" sound, "t" a "d" sound, and "e" a "u" sound. The spelling of Chinese placenames and words in this volume follows that used while I was in China rather than that of the currently favored Pinyin system. In general, the Pinyin system leads to pronunciations very similar to those we were taught to use, although the spellings in English may be markedly different.

Most Chinese cities have the same names today that they did when I was there. A notable exception is Beijing, the present-day capital city, whose name means "Northern Capital." When the Nationalists gained control of China, they moved the capital to Nanching, which means "Southern Capital," and renamed the Northern city "Peiping," which means something like "Northern Park." In the late forties, the Communists defeated the Nationalists and moved the capital back to Beijing.

As time went on, most of us learned a smattering of the Chinese language over there, and might understand some passages of a conversation with someone speaking in the national dialect, which was called "Peiping hua" (Mandarin). Of course, whatever we said was usually conveyed through an intermediary—the interpreter. It was easy to forget that this was the case and to feel that we were talking directly to the other party, as is the way conversations in this book are set forth. None of the passages were recorded, so of course all conversations are reported as remembered years later.

To keep a diary was strictly against regulations. But I did see my way clear to maintaining a little tabulation showing where I was each night on a trip, how far I had traveled that day, and the mode of transportation.

Date	Destination	Mode of Transportation	Length	Day's Lodging
ITINERARY				
2 June →	Ta-Shun	Sampan	4 hrs	Sampan NG
3 June →	Lim-Keng	Sampan	3 hrs	No RON NG
3 June →	Nan-Tien	2×2 (Hill)	4 hrs	Magistrate
4 June →	Yu-hu	2×2	6 hrs	USNB OK
5 June →	Kau-Lou	2×2	6 hrs	Hostel OK
6 June →	Shui-toh	2×2	8 hrs	Magistrate OK
7 June →	Shan-men	2×2	5 Li	Mag. School
10 June →	Kuan-Mei	2×2	65 Li	Temple
(Japs left preceding 2 afternoon -looted & killed)				
11 June →	Fan-shan	2×2	45 Li	No RON
12 June →	Mah-Chau	2×2	30 Li	Magistrate
13 June →	Crash → Mah-Chau	2×2	24 Li	
14 June →	Crash → Mah-Chau	2×2	24 Li	
15 June →	Chiang-Chih-Ling	2×2	70 Li	No RON
16 June →	Ping-yang	Canal/Sampan	90 Li	Night NG
17 June →	Juian	Canal/Sampan	40 Li	No RON
7 June →	Lou-toh	Sampan	70 Li	Sampan

I wrote rather lengthy letters home describing my experiences. In these I was not permitted to include any reference to names of places or of other personnel. After I returned to the States my mother turned over to me a packet of all these letters. And by consolidating these two sources of research data, I generated a much more valid picture of things that happened than could have been done by relying on my memory alone.

Many of my friends and neighbors contributed strongly to the preparation of this book. The efforts of Virginia and Ralph Jenkins in editing the manuscript were invaluable, particularly since Ralph was an intelligence officer on the admiral's staff while the flagship of the Seventh Fleet was moored in the Whangpoo River when I was in Shanghai. The painstaking work done by Barry Snidow of Northlake College in resuscitating old photographs is gratefully acknowledged. Marian Veach, who has traveled in China recently, has given me a broad insight into current conditions in that country by giving me a subscription to *China Today*.

Special thanks are due to Barbara and Jack Fryrear of Irving for introducing me to the Trinity Arts Writers Association, whose forthright critiques contributed immensely to the quality of the manuscript.

Jane Akkala of Big Bay, Upper Michigan, contributed greatly with her diligent proofreading of the manuscript.

And finally, grateful recognition is extended to Bea Wentzel of Big Bay who provided a home with electricity for our typewriter while it ground out the final version of the manuscript during the months Maggie and I lived in our primitive cabin high on a cliff overlooking Lake Superior.

PROLOGUE

WASHINGTON BUREAUCRAT AND

TACTICAL AIR INTELLIGENCE

"We're at war!" yelled the boys at the Syracuse airport. "The Japanese have bombed Pearl Harbor." I had just landed my trusty Piper J-5 after a training flight. As a student pilot I was flying S-turns and figure eights while my nation's fleet was being savaged.

So at last we were in it too! More than two years had passed since Hitler invaded Poland and more than four years since the Japanese assaulted Shanghai. The British were parceling out their national treasure to buy American war goods, and this was bringing about abatement of the long, grinding depression which had resisted everyone's efforts to shake it off.

Although I have long considered myself to be a naturalized Texan, I was born in Flint, Michigan, which at the time was a fine county seat and local market center. My father found various sales jobs in the automobile industry and during my school days my family moved quite frequently to towns in Ohio and Michigan. We finally settled in Birmingham, Michigan, where I went through high school. It was a wonderful country town with aspirations of becoming a city, but it never made it while I was there because under state law a city had to have a population over five thousand. During summer vacations I worked in the building construction industry and went with my family on prolonged camping trips into the wilderness areas of Northern Ontario. Perhaps this instilled a spirit of adventure in me.

Having a strong bent toward engineering, I entered the Mechanical Engineering School at Cornell University, graduating in June, 1932, at the lowest ebb of the Great Depression. Every year before then, major companies had sent representatives to Ithaca to interview engineering graduates, and each of them could be assured of receiving at least three offers. Not a single interviewer showed up for my class. Michigan was probably the hardest hit area in the country, so I stayed in Ithaca and found a rough job as a construction laborer. The county badly needed a new courthouse and jail, and I joined the campaign to get the job done while construction costs were at rock bottom lows. The project was approved and I hired on as a laborer. Pretty soon the field engineer, who had had much better assignments, suddenly quit, and I became field engineer when there was such work to be done.

Unfortunately we completed the courthouse job and I had to go back to Michigan for the worst few months of my life. Nothing was stirring there. Finally I located a job in New York State and then another in New York City. One day my boss tried to get out of paying me and I quit, having no idea what I might do next. I went back to my rooming house. The telephone down the hall rang for me. "This is the American Radiator Company. Would you be interested in a job with us as a designer-draftsman?"

"Yes."

"When can you be available?"

"I'll be there in twenty minutes."

Two years later I got a better job with Carrier Corporation, the pioneers of air conditioning, and spent six good years with them. By the time of Pearl Harbor I was quite comfortably situated as a development engineer. My work recently had been on equipment for the military, but I had no thought of seeking deferment as an essential cog in a wheel of the American industrial complex. No, I was young, healthy, single and adventurous, with a yen to be in on some of the action. My longstanding enthusiasm for aviation had sent me out to the airport for flying lessons as soon as I could afford them.

With the war under way, I received my private pilot license. The military didn't see fit to enroll applicants of my advanced age—over thirty—as flight cadets, and besides I had to wear corrective lenses, so I applied for duty in aeronautical engineering. The navy granted me a commission in the Naval Reserve with the rank of Lieutenant, Junior Grade, and ordered me to report to Naval Training School, Massachusetts Institute of Technology, for an intensive four-month course in aeronautical engineering.

During my time at MIT I came across a display model of an advanced fighter-type aircraft. Its sleek lines fascinated me. It obviously had a huge propeller and a giant engine behind it. Its inverted gull wing gave it a particularly clean look. I was told that the model was of the F4U, called the "Corsair."

After finishing the "cram" course at Cambridge, I was ordered to report to the VF Design Branch, Engineering Division, Bureau of Aeronautics, Washington, D.C. "VF" is navy lingo for Fighter Type Aircraft. The Bureau's organization included similar branches for each class of Naval Aircraft, such as torpedo bombers, dive bombers, etc. These branches were generally called "class desks." This duty was hardly what I had in mind the day I applied for a commission, but "orders is orders." And once there, I started learning about the history of the Corsair. The XF4U-1 had flown four hundred miles per hour in 1940! The navy possessed a world beater. Rex Beisel, the designer, had gone all out for performance. The configuration featured an inverted gull wing which gave it a short lightweight landing gear and a favorable juncture of wing and fuselage. The armament was four machine guns, two in the fuselage and one in each wing. The pilot sat well forward where he had a good view of runways and landing signal officers. All fuel was carried in wing tanks.

The delighted navy awarded the Chance Vought Aircraft Company a production contract. Of course, there would be a few changes. To start with, six fifty-caliber machine guns would be installed in the wings. This took up space where fuel tanks had been located. So Vought placed a monster fuel cell in the fuselage where the pilot had been, and moved the pilot way aft to a spot where his visibility was marginal at best. The weight of the pilot and his cockpit moved the center of gravity farther aft than anyone thought it should be, but this condition could be lived with.

The navy wanted greater quantities than Vought could furnish, so it brought Goodyear Aircraft Company and Brewster Aeronautical Corporation into the picture to manufacture their versions of the Vought design. More than sixty-two hundred Corsairs were eventually delivered to the navy, as well as more than twenty-four hundred to Great Britain and New Zealand under the lend-lease program.

As the navy became more familiar with the airplane, it learned that in its quest for all-out performance Vought had treated many operational problems rather cavalierly. Powerful elements in the navy decided that the Corsair was not suited for carrier operations, and that they should rely solely on the more pedestrian front line fighter, the Grumman F6F Hellcat. The earlier Corsairs were allocated to the British Fleet Air Arm and to the Marine Corps. The British used them with great success on their aircraft carriers, possibly because the British carrier landing doctrine, which was basically to grease the airplane onto the deck hot and low, accommodated the peculiarities of the early bouncy Corsairs better than ours, which was to fly at just above a power stall twenty-five over the deck, chopping the throttle when the landing signal officer called for a "cut." The airplane would then drop to the deck in a controlled crash. The British system was catastrophic when the ship heaved just before the airplane reached the fantail.

With its rearward center of gravity and its beautifully designed ailerons, the F4U was always a nimble airplane. Its clean aerodynamics assured that it would be a stable gun platform.

Unexpectedly, after I had been in the Bureau a short time, I was named Class Desk Officer for the Vought-Brewster-Goodyear program, and for most of the next two years devoted six long days a week to processing engineering changes, more than six hundred of them, through the ponderous bureaucracy. Oh, there were frequent interruptions during which I rode in or flew SNJs, JRBs and DC-3s to naval air stations from Connecticut to Florida and from Norfolk to San Diego. It was all wearing duty, involving decisions such as, "How many combat pilots can we sacrifice to save the lives of twenty kids in the training commands?" This was playing God. Making such decisions all day is not conducive to sleeping well at night. As a lieutenant I did not, of course, have final say in these matters. But except for one minor instance, every change went the way I had decided it should go.

My skipper, Commander (and quite soon, Rear Admiral) John Pearson strongly supported the Corsair. He predicted, "Before the war is over, the F6F will be hopelessly outclassed by the oncoming Japanese fighters. Our only prospect for maintaining air superiority lies in the F4U." He demanded that the navy stick with the airplane until its deficiencies and problems were all corrected. In my opinion, Pearson played an indispensable role in bringing the Corsair to its ultimate glory.

The power of the engine was gradually increased from eighteen hundred to twenty-four hundred horsepower. The three-bladed propeller was replaced with a four-bladed. The pilot's seat was raised some eight inches, and was finally given a full bubble canopy instead of the 1940 model "bird cage." A special task force comprising navy and contractor personnel conducted extensive tests on a Corsair and worked out a modified procedure for servicing the landing gear so that it became more "oleo" and less "pneumatic," alleviating the tendency to make extremely bouncy landings.

The airplane sometimes wallowed during landing runouts. Student pilots, tapping brakes the way they had been trained to in the advanced trainers, quite frequently flipped the airplane over on its back in crashes that all too often were fatal. The marines, at one of their training stations, worked out a fix that extended the tail wheel six inches more. This elevated the airplane out of the attitude that caused wallowing.

A bulkhead behind the pilot was sealed to protect him from engine exhaust fumes, which entered the cut-out for the tail wheel and the hook and worked their way forward.

By the latter part of 1944 most of the badly needed changes had been processed through the system and Vought had brought out a new version, the F4U-4, which was truly the superb fighter that Pearson had envisioned years before. It appeared to me that the work I was still doing wouldn't have much of an impact on the war effort. I was ready for a change of duty.

My friend, Lieutenant Sullivan, in the Production Division of the Bureau, asked me, "Why don't you put in for field duty with Technical Air Intelligence? TAI people prowl around outlandish places, sending out reports on enemy airplanes. They have some fabulous experiences."

What was Technical Air Intelligence all about? One aspect is illustrated by the following story concerning the time in 1942 when the US Army Air Corps took over air warfare in China from the American Volunteer Group (AVG). The Network had reported a formation moving in from the north. An American fighter pilot climbed away from his strip with his engine at maximum allowable manifold air pressure. He spotted the bandits, now east of where he expected to find them, and closed rapidly. He picked out his first intended victim, and while he was still at extreme range, squeezed his trigger. His fifties failed to fire. He turned aside to operate his electric gun charger. The guns fired now. He closed again, getting on the tail of the closest Japanese. He fired a burst at long range. Both planes were turning. He missed the deflection shot. Moving in behind the enemy airplane, he was about to fire again when the Japanese went into a very tight climbing turn to the right. He tried to follow. The enemy easily turned inside of him. In just moments he realized that his foe was now on his tail and high. He heard what sounded like explosions as three rounds slammed into his armor. Apparently another round penetrated his fuel cell and petalled the aluminum outer layer, holding the wound open. Smoke filled his cockpit and he saw flames around his feet. The Japanese must have put a round somewhere into his coolant system because his cylinder head temperature skyrocketed upward. His plane no longer responded properly to pressure on the stick. He was crippled and on fire. He lost consciousness as his plane arced over into a nearly vertical terminal dive. What had he done wrong? Hadn't he followed exactly the doctrine that had been drilled into him at the training base back in the States? This is the type of problem that Technical Air Intelligence dealt with daily.

Claire Lee Chennault, a civilian who had retired from the Army Air Corps in 1937 with the rank of captain, should have been honored as the father of modern technical air intelligence. But he was a maverick who was usually on the outs with the army hierarchy. He spent several years formulating plans for a group of American volunteer pilots who would fight as mercenaries to defend the Chinese from the invading swarm of Japanese aircraft. China had adequate funds to pay for it all. The only fighters Chennault could find to buy were one hundred Curtiss-Wright P-40 Tomahawks originally scheduled for delivery to the British. He studied everything he could about this model. It was rugged, armored, fitted with self-sealing fuel cells, well-armed, and with its twelve-cylinder inverted V Allison engine, it was moderately fast for its day. Neither its rate of climb nor its rate of turn were impressive.

Chennault studied equipment salvaged from Japanese airplanes that had crashed in China. An intelligence officer attached to the US embassy there recognized the value of this salvage as a prime source of data for technical intelligence. In 1939 the Chinese captured a Nate intact. Chennault flew it through extreme service and combat capability tests, comparing it to contemporary American and British fighters.

Chennault spent months contriving a fighter doctrine to fit the situation which was going to be faced by the forthcoming American Volunteer Group in China. The essence of this doctrine was to use the strong points of your equipment to exploit the weaknesses of the enemy's equipment. The basic tactic was to make a high speed pass in a dive, preferably out of the sun, fire a burst, and then dive on out of the enemy's effective response range. This tactic was fabulously successful early in the war. Later, when the Japanese had much heavier, faster fighters such as the Frank, its use would have been disastrous. TAI was never static.

An Army-Navy-British technical air intelligence organization grew up with units in all theaters of war. One indication of the importance attached to TAI by the military was that TAI personnel were granted high air priorities for travel to their duty stations, sometimes more than halfway around the world. ·

I took Sullivan's advice and contacted the Technical Air Intelligence

Office. The officer to whom I spoke said, "We'd be glad to have you aboard pending a release from your present billet." My commanding officer at the time said, "Surely I'll release you—as soon as you find a qualified replacement." I visited naval air stations up and down the east coast without finding anyone suitable. Finally I thought of my good friend, Lyman Josephs, who had gone through the course at MIT in my class, was eminently qualified, and was already in the Bureau, in the Structures Branch. It was relatively easy to find a replacement for him, so I soon became a TAI officer. My first duty was to attend a six-week course at the Technical Air Intelligence School, at the Anacostia Naval Air Station in Washington, D.C. Our class included both United States and British personnel.

At that time, most Americans liked to think that all Japanese products were second-rate and shoddy, made by cheap labor. We learned at TAI School that Japan's best engineers and production personnel rivaled the best of any other country's. When their first team, small though it might be, took on a project, the results could be spectacular. For instance, early in the war, TAI acquired a Japanese copy of a Sperry autopilot, and sent it to the Sperry people on Long Island, whose engineers were amazed to find that the copy was just as good as their own. The Japanese proceeded to redesign their autopilot. When the TAI people acquired one of these new, improved models, they found it to be superior to anything Sperry had done at the time.

Every enemy airplane, its engine, and each of its accessories carried a nameplate giving the manufacturer's name, the date of manufacture, and a serial number. The nameplates were commonly attached with small aluminum rivets. The TAI field teams would shear off the rivet heads with little cold chisels and scratch the serial number of the airplane on the back with an awl. Airplane serial numbers were coded, but the code was so simple that a child could have broken it. All nameplates were rushed back to Washington by the fastest means available. The nameplates from an individual airplane had only limited intelligence significance. But a panel of experts in Washington, headed by a Royal Australian Air Force lieutenant colonel, organized the information given on nameplates from all over into a compilation which generated a record

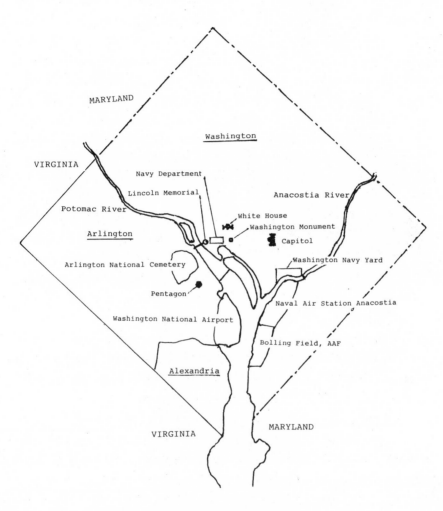

District of Columbia 1945
(Map by Byron Winborn)

Photo of Winborn taken in
Washington.

of the production of each airplane, engine and accessory plant in Japan

As intelligence people say, "Put each little dot in the right place and the picture emerges." The lead time for each component became apparent and any critical bottlenecks were highlighted. Such bottlenecks became prime targets for bomber commands operating in the Pacific. The compilation showed that after one memorable raid, production at a target plant continued without interruption. Production at another plant, a mile away and not critical, stopped abruptly and then slowly recovered over the next few months. Bombardiers were only human.

Rather late in the war a high-ranking US staff officer learned how much TAI valued finding dated nameplates. So, with profound military logic, he ordered, "The dates on all American aircraft nameplates shall be mashed into illegibility, effective at once." Of course, the Japanese hadn't been bombing our factories, even though they may have collected a lot of nameplate dates. But the next time TAI's Japanese counterparts worked over a crashed American airplane, they spotted the mashed dates and said, "Ah, so!" From then on all dates on existing Japanese aircraft were found to be obliterated, and the date spaces on all future aircraft were left blank. Americans had a talent for creating problems for themselves.

TAI personnel called nameplates "jamtins" and general instructions to TAI field teams commonly included a request to send in more jamtins. I wonder if this sly device ever confused the clever adversaries who intercepted our dispatches.

The instructors at the TAI School taught us to identify all Japanese airplane models by their appearance and how to distinguish a Nakajima engine from a Mitsubishi at a distance; also to know enough of the written language to translate the information set forth on nameplates. We learned military ranks, ratings and insignia. Classified bulletins giving detailed descriptions of all Japanese airplanes, engines, and armaments were issued to each of us.

The school's instructors lectured us concerning tropical and oriental diseases and how, hopefully, to avoid contracting them. They coached us in the rudiments of hand-to-hand combat, saying, "Forget the Marquis of Queensbury rules. Concentrate on dislocating shoulders, strangling, and gouging out eyes." A field assignment in TAI did not constitute combat duty, but it might well mean duty in combat areas.

TAI field teams were trained to work rapidly—a downed airplane might attract just the wrong class of people. The 3M Corporation in Minnesota furnished a masking tape with a glossy outer surface having alternate black and white squares, each one-inch long. When a TAI team first got to its quarry, it would run this tape in all key directions—fore and aft on the fuselage, around its girth, out to the wing tips, around the wing sections, across the propeller, and all over the empennage. Then it would snap a lot of photographs. Someone back in Washington would get to count all of the squares and find out what the dimensions of the plane had been.

The instructors told us, "Retrieve the crystals in the radios so that our side will know what frequencies the bad guys are using. [Their pilots always beat me to this one]. Harvest the jamtins, make rubbings of the markings on the guns, collect one sequence of ammo, and look particularly carefully for anything new."

Toward the end of the course, one of the officers at the TAI Center at Anacostia showed me a map of China and pointed out a town called Linhai. It was on the southeast coast, a short distance below Shanghai. At the time, all of the media in the States reported Japanese forces to be in control of the eight hundred miles of the Yangtze River Valley that stretch from the China Sea to the Yangtze Gorges, most of China north of the stretch, Manchuria, Korea, the southern half of the Sakhalin Islands, the Kurile Islands, Okinawa and the rest of the Ryuku Islands, Formosa, Iwo Jima, part of the Marianas, all of the Caroline Islands,

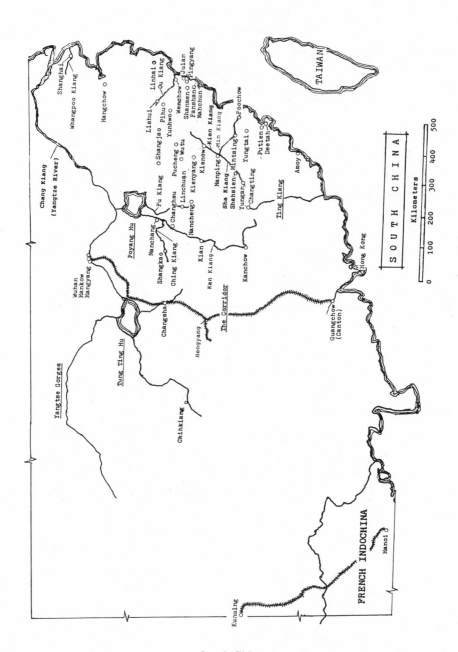

South China
(Map by Byron Winborn, based on maps given to him by
First Lieutenant Russel D. Martinko, USA)

New Ireland, Bougainville, Western New Guinea, the Philippines, the vast Netherlands East Indies, Singapore and the Malay States, Hainan Island, French Indochina, all of Burma, the southeastern part of India, and all of the major ports on the Southeast China coast—Shanghai, Hangchow, Ningpo, Wenchow, Foochow, Amoy, Swatow, Hong Kong and Canton. A Japanese general might have flown some seven thousand miles east and west, and some five thousand miles north and south, remaining over territory he controlled all the way.

The Allies could still fly tonnage from northeastern India over the Hump to their huge base at Kunming, Yunnan Province, China, and to Chungking and Chengtu in Szechuan Province. Six-by-six trucks and four-by-four Jeeps and weapons carriers could move supplies overland to service guerrilla activities, intelligence outposts, and weather and coastwatcher stations in Southeast China. Airplanes with venturesome pilots could fly high priority items and personnel out to strips such as Kweilin and Liuchow in Kwangsi Province, Hengyang and Chihkian and Hunan Province, and Kanchow further east in Kiangsi Province. Most of these strips were former AVG fields.

In the summer of 1944 the Japanese mounted a big drive which captured a corridor along the railway running southward from the Triple Cities on the Yangtze River, through Changsha in Hunan Province and down to Canton in Kwangtung Province on the South China Coast. Kweilin, Liuchow, Hengyang and other South Central China cities also fell. All allied surface-traffic routes were severed, but trucks and Jeeps left stranded east of the corridor could still operate over the remaining atrocious mountain roads in Southeast China. Brave and resolute pilots could fly over the corridor and, with luck, still bring mail, personnel, and very high priority material into and out of Kanchow. Food, gasoline, oil, cigarettes and liquor were not high priority material.

And then in December, 1944, a major enemy drive stalled out just short of Kanchow and cut off all traffic to Southeast China. With prodigious effort an emergency strip at Changting, Fukien Province, still farther east, was improved to the extent that air logistics could be resumed. Flights were occasionally made to other strips such as Kienow,

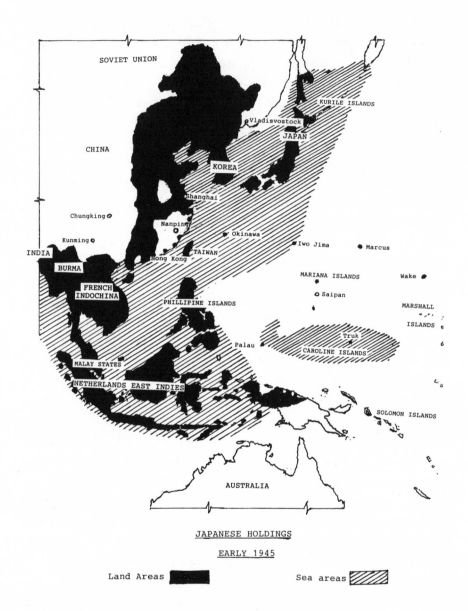

JAPANESE HOLDINGS

EARLY 1945

Land Areas ███████   Sea areas ▨▨▨▨

(Map by Byron Winborn)

farther to the north. Southeast China was officially construed to be occupied territory.

The might of the Japanese empire denied access to the area from the north, from the south, and from routes across the Pacific. It was the land out there that was reached only at the end of a long, hard trip traveling eastward.

The conglomeration of outfits operating in this area included the predominantly powerful Japanese Army with its many garrisons, the US Navy's Sino-American Cooperative Organization, Chinese troops, including many trained by SACO (pronounced "Sock-O"), General Tai Li's secret police, assorted American intelligence and rescue units, TAI, Changting Air Force Base, weather stations, Christian missionaries, Office of War Information (OWI) personnel, Colonel Bill Donovan's Office of Strategic Services (OSS—the forerunner of the Central Intelligence Agency), US Department of State representatives, a British Military Mission, dissident Chinese, Japanese puppets, organized bandit clans, the Chinese War Area Service Corps (WASC) which operated hostels, and who knows what else?

Many of the Americans there felt that an unstated reason for continuing to operate in Southeast China, and indeed in all of China, was to keep the country from collapsing completely after so many years of disastrous warfare. It is not generally realized, but more Japanese troops were pinned down in China at the end of the war than our forces ever encountered in the Pacific. And while their troops in China were generally not of the highest caliber, they would have made our situation vastly graver if they had been unleashed against us. And China would surely have collapsed if it had not been for American support, even though much of the time this support was only moral.

The same TAI officer who had showed me Linhai on the map of China told me, "The TAI Center just received a detailed report on a Japanese airplane which crashed near Linhai. Our field officer was on the spot."

So I volunteered for duty in Southeast China, where only volunteers were sent.[1]

All naval personnel going to China were given lessons on how to act in that country by an office in Washington called the Interior Control Board, a title which revealed to outsiders absolutely nothing indicating what its function might be. The ICB coached us on how to get along with our host ally, giving tips such as, "Always refer to them as the Chinese and never as Chinamen," and "Don't be surprised if a Chinese darts in front of your speeding Jeep to cut off his demon for the day."

I finished the TAI course, took final leave, and received orders to fly to Kunming, China, with a Class II Priority (high), report to the TAI Unit, HQ 14th Army Air Force, and travel as directed by this unit. I was told, "In the meantime, never be away from your telephone for more than one hour, pending further instructions."

---

[1] Years later Lieutenant Commander Gillingham, who had been in my class at Anacostia, told me, "The fellows in our class who did not volunteer for duty in some specific area, generally hazardous, were assigned to a pool at Pearl Harbor. From there, three of them were sent ashore in the third wave at Iwo Jima. They sought cover in a shell hole. Another shell hit the same spot and wiped them all out." I decided that selecting China duty hadn't been a bad idea.

1

Flight Halfway

AROUND

THE WORLD

$\mathbf{M}$y telephone came through with the message I had been waiting for. "Board the R4D leaving Washington National Airport for Naval Air Station Patuxent River at 1730 hours today. Proceed as directed at PAX."

One of my friends drove me and my gear over to the airport. A chief petty officer, Orville E. Millard, ACMM, of the Technical Air Intelligence Center, Anacostia, was being sent to China with me. His orders directed him to stay with me at all times. My orders said nothing about him, but that was fine with me.

After the short hop to Patuxent, we were put aboard a Douglas Skymaster that took off for Port Lyautey, Morocco, with scheduled stops at Stephenville, Newfoundland, and the Azores. In Port Lyautey we got our first sack time in three days. The US Air Force flew us on to Oran and Algiers—very French.

I was billeted in Algiers with a couple of marine officers in a US Air Force hostel that had been a small French hotel. We were served dinner, very tasty, but food was scarce in Algiers and the servings were tiny. Still hungry, one of us said, "Let's go out on the town and look for a French restaurant." We passed several stores selling *eau de vie* before we found a place to eat. It had no menu—everything was *table d'hote*. The first course was turnip soup. We couldn't help wondering how long

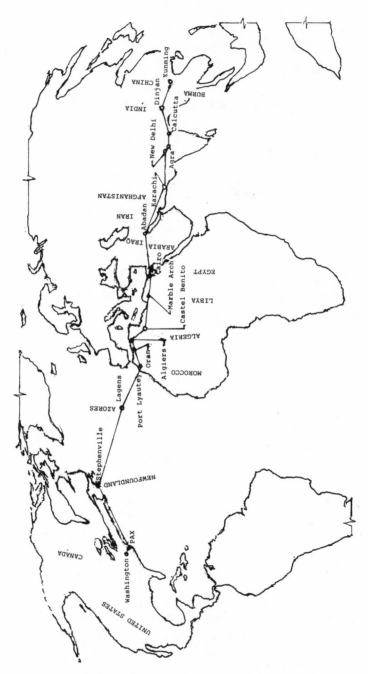

Washington to Kunming—Halfway around the World
(Map by Byron Winborn)

it had been since the restaurant had acquired a whole turnip. The entree was camel liver with French bread. The bread was excellent. Apparently fuel too was scarce in Algiers, because the liver seemed to be quite rare. One of the marines, who had been a gunny sergeant for many years, stuck a fork into the liver and exclaimed, "Well, at least you know it's not rotten when the blood spurts out like that." Dessert was delicious, a locally grown tangerine.

The next day, a British Dakota carried us on east. It was February, the cabin heater was inoperative, and our chilliness wasn't alleviated by the view of the snow-capped Atlas mountains off to the south. That afternoon we swooped down for a landing in front of a desolate shelled-out hanger somewhere in Libya. The crew chief said, "It's time for a spot of tea,"—most welcome since it was piping hot.

We landed at Cairo West after nightfall. It was too dark to see the nearby Pyramids and the Sphinx. After a couple of truck rides we arrived at Paine Field, the US Air Force's large base out in the desert east of Cairo. We asked, "Where can we stow our gear until flight time?"

"No facilities available. Keep it with you."

"Where is the billeting area?"

"Camp Huckstep. Twenty miles out in the desert."

"How do we get there?"

"Get a pass to leave the base and walk out to the main gate. Catch a truck which stops there." The main gate was half a mile away. By the time the truck showed up, more passengers than it could carry were swarming around, so we waited an hour for the next truck.

The billeting sergeant at Camp Huckstep issued us blankets and pillows.

"Where are the barracks?"

"In that large Quonset hut over there."

We stumbled across the sand and gravel to the hut and turned on a light switch. Every light in the place turned on, showing a couple of hundred fellows trying to sleep on cots. They groaned. With our gravelly boots we crunched across the concrete until we found empty cots. Spreading our blankets, we crunched over to the light switch, turned it off, and crunched back in the darkness searching for our own cots. We were just about to sink into a blissful sleep when all lights went on again and the next truckload of transients came crunching in.

We were very happy to get cleared for a flight going east. About an hour out, one of the passengers said, "Wasn't that a magnificent view of Jerusalem!"

"Where?"

"Out the portside windows about twenty minutes ago."

After crossing Saudi Arabia and Iraq, desolate wastelands with an occasional mud hut village, we put in at Abadan, Iran, for a noon-day meal. It was dark by the time we landed at Karachi, a British-run facility, much more obliging than Paine Field.

In the air again, we hopped to New Delhi and on to Agra. It was night and one of the passengers who knew the territory said, "We are now right over the Taj Mahal." It was too dark to see anything.

The base at Agra was operated by the British, who made sure that everything was most accommodating. Our billets were in small tents with wooden decks, brick fireplaces and plenty of natives to shine our shoes.

After three hours of uninterrupted sleep we were routed out and put aboard another airplane. It was daylight by the time we landed at DumDum Field, the aerodrome for the great city of Calcutta.

I was not enough of a world traveler to feel at home in Calcutta. The air of the city carried a distinct aroma compounded of all the effluents of millions of people, cows, cooking fires, spices, burning ghats, and factories. Unlike the immense suburban areas of unbelievable squalor, downtown was most impressive, with wide streets and large stone buildings having no first floor windows. Sacred cows wandered everywhere, and whenever one of them answered the call of nature, some human would scoop up the contribution with his hands, mold it into neat patties, and plaster them in a row on the wall of the nearest building. Some sort of honor system must have been in effect, because when the patties had dried in the sun, the original owner was able to retrieve his own. He placed the chips in a basket on his head and carried them off. They were an ideal fuel for home cooking.

We were billeted more than half a mile from downtown in a US Navy hostel on Karaya Road at its intersection with Sidi bin Amir, or something like that. Upon awakening each morning the first thing we heard was the squawking of flocks of large black birds. Without their diligent scavenging, the airs of Calcutta would really have been pungent.

Walking downtown one morning, I passed a butcher shop with a barrel of offal out front. One of the birds had grabbed the end of a fifteen-foot length of intestine and was trying to fly off with it. A man also wanted it just as badly and was hanging on to the other end. I couldn't tell which was squawking the louder, the man or the bird.

A little farther on I happened to be walking behind a tottery old beggar. Suddenly he collapsed into a heap, rolled his eyes until only the whites showed, and was dead. I was so close behind I had to step over his body. Late that afternoon I walked back on the other side of the street and noticed that the beggar's corpse was still lying there. I had heard that it was strictly against regulations of the Corporation, as the municipal government was called, to leave corpses on the streets for more than twenty-four hours, so I supposed that it would be removed soon.

The urchins on the streets spoke no English, but they had been coached by the American GI's to recite in plaintive tones, "*Baksheesh, Sahib. Baksheesh.* No momma. No poppa. No suppa. No rotation. No per diem. No more Chelseas please. *Baksheesh, Sahib.*" Chelseas were the "low-bidder" cigarettes the US Army furnished us in its C-rations.

One day I went over to a navy depot in town to draw my forty-five automatic and get it out of its cosmolene, a heavy grease-like material with which guns are coated as a means of preservation. An enlisted man was standing several feet from me with a small monkey perched on his shoulder. The monkey eyed me closely, leapt to my shoulder, bit me hard on the elbow and jumped back to his master's shoulder. I couldn't very well reprimand the man for something his monkey had done. It would have been more fitting to commend him for training his pet to identify an officer so positively, which I didn't do either.

An infamous red light district had been located out on Karaya Road, presided over by Margot, reputedly proclaimed in a national publication in the states to be the most notorious madam in the world. The Corporation, the British military, and the American military had collaborated in a drive that completely wiped out the red light district two months before I arrived in town—no connection with my coming, of course.

Quite late one night I stopped at the Great Eastern Hotel for a gimlet or two. I decided that it wouldn't be prudent to walk home in a strange city late at night, and hailed a taxi. As far as I could tell, all taxis were Buick touring cars with loud horns, and all taxi drivers were Sikhs, with long beards tucked beneath their turbans. I said, "Karaya Road and Sidi bin Amir." The driver, an honorable man, refused to take me, explaining, "No Sahib, Karaya Road clos-ed."

So I hailed a ricksha. Once a young man made a career of pulling rickshas in that fetid climate his life expectancy dropped to five years. You didn't have to talk to a ricksha hauler, you just pointed out which way you wanted to go. After that, you steered him by tapping him gently on the buttock, one side or the other, with the toe of your shoe. We went clop-clopping out dark Karaya Road. Suddenly my puller darted toward a completely unlit alley, where, no doubt, he had colleagues who were not above rolling a rich foreigner. I gave my puller a boot on the buttock that he must have remembered for the rest of his brief life. He resumed course and didn't misbehave again.

After a week of processing, we were cleared for the flight over the Hump and on into Southwest China. The Air Force suffered many casualties on the Hump run because the altitudes of the passes were perilously high and the weather was typically lousy.

The navy sent its personnel into and out of China via the China National Aviation Corporation (CNAC), an airline in which PanAmerican had a forty-five percent interest. Everyone recognized that Japan, too, had to have some way of doing the same. CNAC was the logical route. Rumors hinted that the airline and the Japanese had a quiet little agreement under which CNAC would board any passenger cleared by the British in Calcutta or the Chinese in Kunming without checking his character. In return, the Japanese did not molest CNAC planes flying over their bases in Burma. This afforded a more southerly route over the

Himalayas, with passes at lower elevations and better weather than our Air Force had to contend with on its Hump runs. In any event our navy got several thousand of its personnel into China without a single casualty while our Air Force lost three thousand people on its Hump fights.

Even though we had no idea how long we might be in China, or what we might be able to draw from supply once we got there, our baggage weight restriction was most severe. I had to send back to the States a valpack full of uniforms that I had lugged all the way from Washington. I also had to give away a pair of shoes to one of the Indian crew on the truck that took us out to the aerodrome. But anything that we could hang on our persons was exempt from the weight limitation. So each of us wore a heavy coat, an escape vest, a pistol, a web belt full of ammunition, a canteen, a sheath knife, a first aid kit, and a gas mask. Taking off from Dinjan in northeastern India in a C-47, we rode all night sitting upright in bucket seats, much of the way at sixteen thousand five hundred feet, gasping for air while the crew up forward was on oxygen, for which we were thankful. The next morning, in broad daylight, we came in for a landing at Kunming, one hundred and eighty degrees of longitude around the world from Washington.

China at last! How did we feel? Mostly we felt beaten up by a long series of night flights in bucket seats, and quite conscious of the twelve-hour time difference. Of course Kunming was in Southwest China, but we felt sure we would arrive at our final destination in a few more days.

2

KUNMING:

PROCESSING FOR DUTY

IN SOUTHEAST CHINA

Kunming had perhaps the busiest airport in the world in early 1945. The long strip was constructed of stone, broken up with handheld hammers, distributed in baskets hanging from yoyo poles, and compacted with huge wooden rollers hauled by a couple hundred coolies. The base was on a large plateau at 6240 feet elevation. This made the air thin enough so that airplane landing speeds were noticeably faster than we were accustomed to. The February weather was cold at night and warm enough at noon for sunbathing.

We could hear the roar of airplanes almost continuously and see the clouds of dust kicked up by the C-46 transports taxiing to and from their parking areas. Occasionally someone who had access to a Jeep would say, "Let's go into town for dinner at a Chinese restaurant." Delicious! That was more than could be said for the chow served on the base.

I spent seven days being processed for duty with the TAI Unit, Nanping, Fukien Province, in occupied Southeast China. A military pass signed by General Chennault extended to me and my party "Every possible aid insofar as consistent with other military requirements." You might say that I could have anything I asked for so long as nobody else wanted it.

HEADQUARTERS, FOURTEENTH AIR FORCE
A. P. O. 627, C/O POSTMASTER
NEW YORK CITY, NEW YORK

24 February 1945

SUBJECT: Technical Air Intelligence.

TO   : All Armed Forces within the China Area.

1. The bearer of this letter, BYRON R. WINBORN, JR., 207076, Lt., A-V(S), USNR, whose photograph and signature appear below, is a Technical Air Intelligence Inspector for the Fourteenth Air Force. He and his unit are to take complete charge of all crashed or captured enemy air equipment as early as possible. Every possible aid will be given this officer and his party, consistent with other military requirements.

2. It is directed that all necessary transportation, communication facilities, guard, rations, labor, shipping materials, vehicle fuels, parts, supplies, and other required assistance be supplied upon his request insofar as consistent with other military requirements.

C. L. CHENNAULT,
Maj. Gen. U.S.A.,
Commanding General,
14th Air Force.

SIGNATURE OF BEARER

Pass from Headquarters, Fourteenth Air Force,
signed by Major General C. L. Chennault

Each American was given a Chinese name that was a transliteration in Chinese characters, which when spoken sounded something like his name in English. I contacted a young Chinese who had an excellent command of the English language and asked him to suggest a Chinese name for me. He came up with "Wen Bon," typically pronounced "Wunbun."

I agreed, "That's closer to my name than most of the transliterations I've heard around here."

I had been told that a less than friendly transliterator could generate a phrase which had some subtle hidden connotation of the most unfortunate type. So I asked, "Please explain what 'Wen Bon' means."

"It means 'original literature.'"

I had learned that few phrases could be translated exactly from one language to the other, so I asked, "Could you give me an expanded interpretation of 'original literature'?"

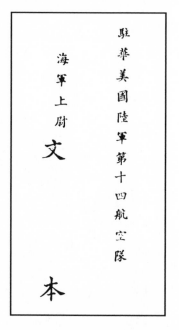

"Yes. The 'original' is the character 'bon' used in 'Jih Bon,' the 'Land of the Rising Sun' to indicate emerging or original."

"I am not enthused about having part of Japan in my name."

"The character 'bon' is widely used elsewhere."

"OK. What about the 'literature'?"

"Wen is a well-known Chinese surname. Perhaps its best interpretation is the word 'pen' in the phrase 'the pen is mightier than the sword.'"

"Very good. Thank you."

I ordered calling cards showing my name, rank, and "American 14th Air Force" all in Chinese. Then I had a small neat stone chop, or stamp, made with "Wen

Winborn's calling card, "Beautiful Country Sea Force; Highest Level of Low Ranking Officers; Wen Bon"

Bon" and characters for "his chop" carved on it. This chop would serve as my legal signature anywhere in China.

I had an interview with a medical officer. The first thing he did was to take the GI medicine kit that had been issued to me and throw away the chlorazone tablets. "Chlorazone," he said, "is for purifying drinking water in other theaters of war. In China every drop of water that you drink or use to brush your teeth must have been boiled. That is the only way to kill the dysentery bugs." Drinking water was called leng kai shui meaning cooled, boiled water.

"Take your atabrine every day when you are on a trip," the medical officer continued. "Your skin will turn a garish yellow just like all the other Americans. But malaria symptoms, chills and fever will be suppressed. When you return to base, discontinue the atabrine. If malaria symptoms then appear, get yourself flown to Kunming on the next flight for treatment with quinine." Quinine was in critically short supply because the Japanese controlled the areas in the East Indies from which it came.

I knew that soon I would be spending most of my time on prolonged field trips. Another step in my processing was to arrange for my travel expenses. I was duly constituted a Class B Finance Agent of the United States Army. Why the Army? Well, they were allies and besides they had a procedure set up for handling travel expenses. As part of the routine involved, I was interviewed by a serious-minded Army Finance Officer— a captain.

Official Chinese National money was denominated in yuan, but we never used that term. Instead we spoke of Chinese money as so many dollars CN, written, for example, as "$100 CN." Amounts in US currency were referred to as so many "dollars gold." Out where I was headed, US currency was unknown so all cash transactions, including my pay, would be in CN.

It was determined that I should be entrusted with a stipulated amount of Chinese money, $300,000 CN. I was issued a pad of voucher sheets. Each time an allowable travel expense was incurred, an appropriate entry was to be made on the current voucher sheet showing the date, location, item of merchandise or service provided, amount, and vendor's or provider's signature, or, if he couldn't write, his right thumbprint. From time to time, a filled-out voucher would be sent back to Kunming and my balance would be restored.

I asked the finance officer, "What is the extent of my personal liability for the Army's funds?" He said, "You will not be held personally liable for any loss provided that reasonable precautions are exercised to safeguard the funds." Somewhere or other I found a stout, little, steel box nine and one-half inches long, which once had served as a first aid kit. I went to the flea market in downtown Kunming and bought a combination lock made in Germany and a cheesy hasp. The hasp was riveted to the box at the airplane repair shop on the base.

I made another appointment with the finance officer and showed him the box. He said, "The box will be entirely satisfactory." I asked him for permission to speak "off the record." He replied, "Certainly, Lieutenant." I pointed out, "During the kind of duty facing me it will be quite possible for some thief to make off with the Army's funds, box and all," and asked, "In the event of such an untoward incident, would it be construed that reasonable precautions had been exercised?" "Oh yes," he said. "There are limits to the extent of the precautions the Army expects you to take."

The captain was doing all that he could to make me a good Class B Finance Agent.

I learned other lessons, too, while in Kunming. An M1 carbine stood in the corner of the War Area Service Corp's adobe hostel where I was billeted. WASC was a Chinese contribution to the war effort. I picked up the gun. It felt good. I brought it up to my shoulder and drew a bead on a canteen on a high shelf across the room. I squeezed the trigger.

CRACK!

Water spouted from a thirty caliber hole. My only consolation was that the hole was precisely in the center of the target. The canteen had been issued to a lieutenant named Statler. I handed my canteen, issued to me in Calcutta, over to Statler. This was a small price to pay for learning that all guns in China were loaded unless proven otherwise moments before.

The steel box in which Winborn kept his money while traveling. The
Chinese bill on top of the box is nearly the same size as an American bill.
(Photo by Winborn)

Once out in the field I bought a few Chinese glass bottles with
pithy stoppers. They were better than canteens anyway—they didn't
impart a metallic taste to the water.

Kunming was situated in open terrain. Several villages could be
sighted far away in various directions. The wind was fresh most of the
time. Sometimes you would detect a definite odor, not a stench, but
something musty and unpleasant. Facing directly into the wind, you
would find yourself looking straight toward one of the villages. A few
minutes later the odor would vanish—the wind's direction had changed
by a few degrees.

One afternoon Lieutenant Warren T. Ellis, USNR, of the TAI
headquarters unit at Kunming, took a long walk with me out onto the
plateau. Finding an elaborate stage built to honor some hero or dignitary,
we climbed up and had our pictures taken.

The area was farmed intensively, with an ancient irrigation system
having one set of canals for bringing water in and another set for draining

Village on the plains near Kunming (Photo by Winborn)

it off so as to preclude building up soil salinity. We were beside one of the canals when someone quite near us fired a rifle. We took cover until we discovered that some Chinese soldiers had whistled a dog out of a village on the other side of the canal, and that one of the soldiers had shot the animal. There would be a feast that night, not anything as choice as properly fattened chow dog, but, after all, few military messes are really gourmet. We had observed the Chinese Army's Service of Supply in operation.

That night one of the Navy Supply Officers in Kunming came over and said, "I hear that you are flying out east tomorrow."

I said, "Yeah."

"Could you do a little something for me?"

"Why sure. I am always glad to do a favor for a supply officer. What is it?"

"I have some guard mail to go out east. It has to be in the custody of a commissioned officer. We'll bring it out to your flight. You can turn it over to King in Changting tomorrow afternoon. It won't be any trouble for you."

My processing in Kunming for duty in occupied Southeast China had been completed.

Winborn making himself at home on a stage set up to honor some visiting Chinese dignitary. (Photo by Ellis)

Sampan in an irrigation canal on the Kunming plateau.
(Photo by Winborn)

Old stone bridge over an irrigation canal out on the plateau in the Kunming area.
(Photo by Winborn)

3

GOING OUT EAST:

A REFUELING STOP

AT CHIHKIANG

My flight was to take off from an outlying strip at Chengkung.
I got there by truck before daybreak. To start with, everyone strapped
on his chute. Our bird was a beaten-up old C-47 transport operated by
the 322d Troop Carrier Squadron. A piece of broken rock from a runway
had zoomed up and put a notch in the leading edge of one of our
propellers. You could bury your thumb in the wound. Back in the States
a hole like that would have grounded the airplane right then. The damaged
prop worked just fine in China.

Our C-47 did not have fancy furnishings like bucket seats. The
passengers could just sit on the deck and hang on to the cargo tie-down
rings.

Pretty soon a navy six-by-six truck drove up with ten dispatch bags
each weighing fifty-five pounds. A supply officer got out and said, "Here
is your guard mail, Mr. Winborn. Please sign the ten receipts."

"Am I allowed to know what is in the bags?" I asked.

"Oh, yes," he said. "Chinese currency for the navy out east."

"How much currency?"

"$80,000,000 CN."

At the prevailing exchange rate (if anyone out there knew what an
American dollar was), I was taking on some $180,000 gold, which was

considerably more cash that I normally carried around even in secure areas.

The officer said, "King will take it off your hands this afternoon. It won't be any trouble for you. Thanks a lot. Good-bye."

Shortly before we took off from Chengkung, someone in the uniform of a British lieutenant colonel drove up and put a small Chinese gentleman aboard our C-47. "Mr. Wu," he said, "is an official of the Chinese Nationalist Government in Chungking. He is going to make an inspection tour of the occupied territory out east."

Mr. Wu wore a long gray robe. He spoke excellent English. During the flight he struck up a conversation with me. At times what he said surprised me. I suspect that he hoped to draw me into leaking bits of information. I don't think that I did, but I'm probably wrong. One thing concerned me. Sometimes Mr. Wu's "l's" seemed to have a "r" sound, which I understood to be a Japanese trait. But if Mr. Wu were really Japanese, he was truly a superb agent.

He told me how the Kunming bankers and their cohorts made big money: "They plant rumors to the effect that the Japanese are about to make a major drive on Kunming." This was plausible; most of the American operations in China were utterly dependent on this base. In spite of its importance, Kunming had minimal ground defense, and the Japanese were firmly entrenched in Indochina, not far away. Mr. Wu explained, "The planted rumors spread like wildfire. The value of the Chinese dollar (*yuan*, if you prefer) plummets. The exchange rate soars— 900, 1000, 1100, 1200, 1300. Finally, the cohorts plant a new crop of rumors. Chiang Kai-shek is moving 85,000 of his crack troops down from shadowing the Chinese Communists in the north. They will take up defensive positions around Kunming. The US Army Air Force is moving in another P-51 squadron. The Japanese realize that the drive would be too costly and have canceled their plans for making it. The Chinese dollar recovers. The exchange rate drops—1200, 1100, 1000, 900. The cohorts, knowing which way the rate will move next, exchange their capital accordingly. The profit is theirs for the taking."

Mr. Wu said, "Feel my upper arm." It felt hard.

"What's there?"

"Gold wire, wrapped around my arm. The *yuan* may become worthless while I am still out east. But even quite small towns have an assayer who can evaluate gold wire, snip off a bit, and arrange to exchange it for local goods and services." I couldn't help but reflect that I was going out east, I didn't know for how long, without any gold wire.

We stood up in the airplane in groups of two or three talking to each other. Sometimes, during a lull in the conversation, I would drift away from Mr. Wu. Pretty soon he would be at my side again with another one of his stories.

At one point, Mr. Wu said, "Consider the case of Generals A and B. Both have similar sectors facing the Japanese lines. Both have about the same resources of men, munitions, and money. So, they are of equal status. Now suppose that the Japanese launch a big drive along the entire front. Since we are just supposing, suppose that General A puts up a strong resistance. Even let us suppose that he stops the Japanese drive in his sector, taking heavy losses. He will send a message to Chungking claiming a great victory. There will be victory banquets and parades in the streets. General A will be a great hero.

"Now suppose that General B fires off a little ammunition and a lot of firecrackers. Suppose that he inflicts a few casualties on the Japanese, but mostly trades off space for time. By and by the Japanese will be straining their supply lines and will decide to stop their drive and consolidate their position. General B will send a message to Chungking claiming a great victory. There will be victory banquets and parades in the streets. General B will be a great hero.

"General B now has much greater resources—men, munitions, and money—than General A. So he is much the greater general. If you were a Chinese general, what would you do?"

Mr. Wu also brought up an old Chinese precept which I have heard elsewhere, "Even though you could, never completely entrap your enemy, but rather always leave him at least one escape route." This precept tends to be difficult for an Occidental to assimilate. I think that I am Oriental enough to do so. As a general, your objective is to get the enemy out of your territory. If he wants to withdraw of his own accord, wonderful. Oh, it is all right to harass him while he withdraws. If his troops were to be completely encircled, they would fight like tigers and inflict many casualties on your men. Even if you could capture all of his troops, then what? You know that you couldn't feed them even if you wanted to. You don't have enough provisions to feed your own men properly. Kill them all, whether while still fighting or as prisoners? Could be; but it is a monumental task to bury a horde of dead soldiers. If you do not bury them . . . ?

"No, let them straggle away with great loss of face."

We had to stop at Chihkiang, an important base just west of the Corridor. (A "j" sound is supposed to be given to the "k," but most Americans pronounced it "Chicky-yang"). The weather thickened and by the time we got there thirteen transports were stacked up in the soup, all (they hoped) at different altitudes. As they say, "There are rocks in the clouds," i.e., steep hills surrounded the instrument flight pattern. In the course of time, we were cleared to land.

We had been manifested on through to Changting and merely wanted to refuel. Our pilot taxied over to the pump and said, "Gas her up, Sergeant. We're flying to Changting this afternoon."

"I'll gas her up for you, Captain, but you ain't flying nowhere this afternoon. We're socked in." He was right. So, after only a few days in China I was stranded at a strange base not far from the Japanese Corridor with $80,000,000 CN in my personal custody.

I found out the name of the base commander, a major, and managed to get him on a field telephone set. He was very harried, with many urgent missions stalled out at his base.

I said, "This is Lieutenant Winborn, USNR, speaking. I need a secure place to stow some guard mail overnight."

"No such facility is on the base."

"Then please furnish me with an armed guard."

"No guards are available."

"I don't want to be too explicit over an open telephone, but under the circumstances I feel it necessary to state that my guard mail is navy currency in a very substantial amount."

He hung up.

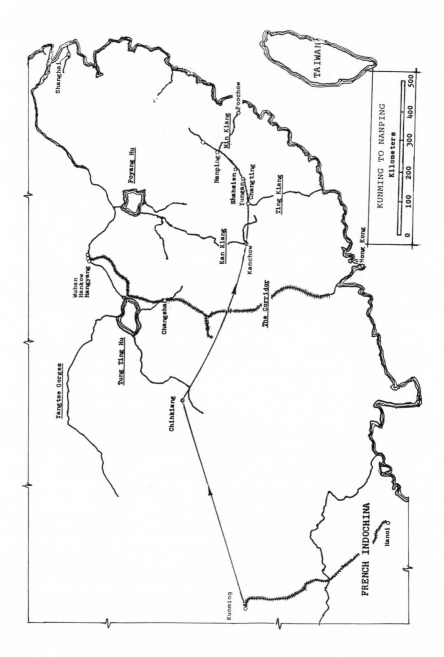

Map by Byron Winborn.

Looking back on this incident many years later, it is clear that I was a prime regulation stuffed shirt. This kind of attitude was permissible and even advantageous in Washington, but Chihkiang was a long way from Washington. The incident marked a turning point in my career. I entered into a prolonged shaping-up process that eventually converted me into what was regarded as a pretty fair operator.

The first step was to locate a likely looking sergeant and tell him what my problem was without exactly saying, "$80,000,000 CN." He said there was space at the Air Freight shack and that a sergeant slept there. The sergeant packed a .45, but of course could not take personal responsibility for my guard mail. The sergeant I was talking to added, "It's your best bet, Lieutenant."

I walked over to Air Freight. The sergeant there agreed to take my guard mail. He asked me where it was now. It was still in our C-47, which had taxied far down the field.

"Do you drive a six-by-six?" the sergeant asked. "There is one right outside."

"Sure."

Actually, I had never been in the cab of this truck. I found a gear that would make it start rolling, and another that would make it go forward pretty well. The ten bags finally got stowed at Air Freight. So I was personally responsible for the navy's ten bags of money stacked in a corner of a shack on an advanced base in China. Everybody had heard rumors about bandits in the country who would risk their lives for $100 CN. I wondered what kind of a story was fated to emerge from this incident? "Lieutenant fights off bandits to save navy's fortune."

After I had stowed my $80,000,000 CN, we slogged our way through the mud to the tent of the billeting sergeant. This individual had been in Chihkiang longer than wars were supposed to last and by now was sublimely immune to life in general and to pleas for billets, blankets and charcoal stoves in particular. We travelers unrolled our sacks on the sloping deck of our transport and set up light housekeeping. The plane was parked in a guarded, restricted area. Mr. Wu told the guards, "We are allies. Do not shoot just because someone coughs in the night."

Someone did cough during the night and the guards all slammed rounds into their Tommy guns and yelled, *"Nah gah!"* Mr. Wu managed to quiet them. There had been a change of the guard.

The Cloak and Dagger Society, mundanely referred to as "Oboe Sugar Sugar," maintained a hostel in the middle of Chihkiang. The very existence of this hostel was a super hush-hush matter known only to about three hundred thousand local Chinese, to the Tai-Li organization, and to an uncounted array of enemy agents, all of whom wore dark glasses. It was even known to a few Americans. One of our passengers was an OSS agent. When he found that we would have to stay over a second night, he spirited Millard and me away to the OSS hostel in Chihkiang. We had been there twenty minutes when Mr. Wu appeared at the door and asked for me. He said, "I am delighted to know that you have found comfortable quarters for your stay in Chihkiang." I did not see Mr. Wu again, but I often thought of things that he had said.

Millard and I settled down to wait for the "Meteorological Miracle of March"—the day when the skies over Chihkiang and over Changting would concurrently be declared auspicious for aviating. As days of the other kind rolled by, it became the custom of a morning to stand upon the crumbling porch of the hostel and scan the overcast that clung moistly to the tiled roofs of Chihkiang. Expert opinion would be voiced as to when, if ever again, the warmth of the sun might seep through to the muds of Hunan Province. Hours were spent discussing whether that thin spot in the overcast—"See, the one over there"—was really getting thinner.

The kids on the streets of Chihkiang would always greet us like conquering heroes, yelling, *"Ding hao!,"* which I understood, and *"Ding qua qua! Qua qua* Joe!," whose meaning was not clear to me. Then invariably they would ask for *tang*, candy.

One morning when our gaze reverted from the skies to the muddy flagstones before the porch, we saw the boy. He was a good-looking kid. He wore the uniform of the Chinese Army and his collar marks proclaimed him to be a superior private. He clutched an ancient watch in one hand and he was obviously on the verge of tears. We greenhorns called out to one of the Americans who spoke Chinese. He gradually informed us, "The soldier is fourteen years old . . . He has been in the army two years . . . The watch belongs to his company commander . . . The commander has ordered him to take it to the watchmaker for repairs and has given him the $200 CN (about forty cents gold) that this will cost . . . On his way, the unfortunate soldier dropped the watch . . . Now it is going to cost $400 CN . . . His company commander will have him beaten if he does not return the watch in good condition . . . Could the Americans please give him the extra $200 CN?"

The Chinese-speaking American was an Old China Hand who had been hardened by a thousand such sob stories—invariably fake. He told the superior private, "It is not the Americans' affair that the watch is broken." The young soldier turned into the little boy that he really was. Tears streamed down his cheeks and he shook with uncontrollable sobs. One of the Chinese fellows attached to the organization handed him the money and he faded away from the compound with his battered watch.

During the rest of my stay in China, I, too, was subjected to countless phony attempts to extract some money from the rich Americans. I turned them all down as a matter of principle, but also later on I witnessed the corporal punishment meted out to Chinese soldiers for minor infractions. If that superior private appeared before me again today, I think that I should give him the $200 CN in spite of my principles.

One day while we were stranded in Chihkiang, the skies cleared enough for local operations. Changting remained closed, according to our radio. We had had what seemed like interminable days of precipitation that seeped downward, upward, sideways and into all crevices. The ignition harnesses of the airplanes on the field were just plain soggy. Nevertheless, an American P-51 pilot managed to get his bird started and running, albeit with a roughness quite unlike the usual sewing-machine purr of a proper Packard-Merlin engine. He succeeded in horsing his airplane into the air—and then his engine cut out and he plunged down. Before he crashed into the ground, his engine picked up again for a few seconds, and he got up to a hundred feet. He could not gain enough altitude to circle around the hill and make an approach to the strip. Nor could he climb high enough to have a chance of making a survivable bail-out.

We spectators on the ground sweated this on-again, off-again struggle for twenty minutes by our watches. Then the engine dried itself out and settled down to its usual continuous roar. The pilot set out on his assigned mission.

That same day, a Chinese pilot coaxed his P-40 into the air with its engine running roughly. Just after lift-off, the engine cut out for the last time. The P-40 arced over into the river just beyond the end of the strip and drove itself beneath the surface. That P-40 carried a five hundred pound bomb. Could the hard impact with the water have armed the bomb? The authorities decided not to risk further loss of life. No divers were sent down.

The American intelligence officers in Chihkiang had to keep in touch with what was going on in the enemy camp across the way. The best source was a Chinese double agent who could prowl around their base freely. Of course, he was an equally good source for them. While we were still there, the double agent reported, "The Japanese have posted a reward of $500 gold for any American officer brought in dead or alive." Our people told the double agent to take back this message: "You cheapskates can go straight to Hell—we are worth at least $1000 gold a head."

Every morning I walked over to Air Freight and patted my money bags. One day I noticed that the strap on one of the bags came loose and the money was visible. Had any been stolen? One thing that I was not going to do was dump it all out on the floor in front of everybody and count it. I simply reattached the strap.

The Air Force Air Transport Command thought nothing of spanning great oceans. However it was distinctly allergic to flying into really hot regions. It might nip into some advance base like Chihkiang, deplane a movie cameraman, and get a little publicity footage on rolling out a Jeep, which showed great courage in a place like that; then it would button up and blast out of that unhygienic area right now, headed west.

The 322d Troop Carrier Squadron would stow about 150 percent of the rated load aboard one of its war-weary C-47s, head east, and stagger forth into skies where sighting another airplane usually meant sighting danger. The 322d had some pretty definite opinions about ATC. When time hung too heavily on our hands we would amble over to 322d Operations and quietly drop some remark about 322d TCS being a branch of ATC. This was guaranteed to banish monotony for about six hours while the air in the shack grew blue with a violent dissertation on the vast distinction between 322d TCS and ATC.

The navy, in those days, had the quaint custom of assigning super naval air priorities to its traveling personnel and then sending them half way around the world on army aircraft, aboard which a naval air priority meant about as much as a New York Central ticket on the Trans-Siberian Railway. Fortunately, most of the Army Priority and Travel Officers and Operations Officers were swell joes who would do just about anything for the navy. But it was a big army, and we never knew quite what might happen.

The 322d Operations Officer at Chihkiang was the salt of the earth. Each day he would receive a dispatch from the commanding general in Kunming assigning priorities down through seven to the various missions stranded at Chihkiang. My mission was never even mentioned. It is doubtful that the general realized that this particular airline of his had hauled us there from Kunming, much less that it had not been able to get us on through to Changting as it was supposed to.

The recommended strategy in a situation like this was to "attach" your mission to one of the missions that enjoyed a definitely superior priority. I attached to the, shall we say, "Hamburger Mission." This admittedly was a pretty transparent device that needed a good break if it were to produce. The break came the day before the weather finally cleared, when the operations officer received a cablegram that had originated in the States two weeks before reading, "YOU ARE NOW THE FATHER OF A SEVEN AND ONE-HALF POUND BOY." He was still in a particularly expansive mood the next day and assigned my mission to the first flight east. So once again the war proceeded in accordance to plan.

I had played a lot of poker with that operations officer during the ten days that we waited on the weather. I didn't seem to be a particularly good poker player. We reloaded my ten bags of money and boarded our trusty C-47 again. The crew chief came aft and said, "OK, fellows, put on your chutes and adjust the harnesses." One of our passengers was a medical officer. He sort of grinned as though to say, "Who ever heard of putting on chutes before they even start the engine?" The rest of us were very much aware of the fact that we were setting out on a flight over enemy-held territory and on into some pretty uncertain real estate. We fussed with the adjustment of our straps until they were just so. Before long the medical officer picked out a chute for himself and put it on. The crew started warming up the engines.

Two large fuel tanks had been installed in the cabin. The cargo and mail were stacked in a great heap on the cabin deck. Four fifty-five gallon drums of aviation gasoline for the return flight were standing on end between the cargo and the fuselage tanks. There were no refueling facilities out where we were going. The piece of flimsy Chinese clothesline, wrapped around the four drums, did very little to inspire confidence that the drums would stay secured if we encountered any little—ah—roughness while taking off.

As soon as our airplane was cleared for take-off the crew chief said, "Let's all move forward, fellows, and give the pilot a break." The medical officer smiled at the thought of passengers on an airliner moving forward for take-off, as though somebody were trying to kid him. The rest of us clambered over the cargo and the four drums, and snuggled around the tanks, grabbing hold of the airplane's structural frames and braces. Finally, the medical officer came forward and joined us.

This was a most propitious time not to have an engine conk out. Neither engine failed. We brushed over those little hills at the end of the strip and staggered up to a bit of altitude. Some time after the flight I learned that our manifest showed a heavy fifty-seven hundred pounds of payload, not including twenty parachutes, a crew of five, and all of that gasoline. Millard and I were both fully-grown men who each weighed about one hundred and eighty pounds. We carried guns, sleeping bags and all of our gear for a tour of indefinite duration. Our commanding officer in Kunming, Major Morris W. Slack, USA, had given us several hundred pounds of supplies, principally photographic materials, to take out to the unit. Of course there was my guard mail, five hundred and fifty pounds of it. Altogether my mission weighed some fifteen hundred pounds, which couldn't very well be shown on the manifest because it hadn't been assigned a priority by the commanding general.

Two other transports joined us and we cruised along just like Sunday afternoon. Our radio picked up two enemy pilots jabbering at each other, but our radar showed that they were miles away. Our fighter escort of four P-51s made great sweeping S-turns around us because they couldn't stay in the air at our pokey speed. The Japanese had the habit of mounting anti-aircraft guns on flat cars and moving the cars on the rail line to new locations in the Corridor each night. One of our fighters would streak down the rail line to find where they were this morning, and minutes later come racing back to lay a slipstream right in front of our nose for us to fly into with a bump. The Mustang was truly a thing of beauty— beauty that was never fully appreciated until it was viewed through the window of a transport lumbering along over enemy territory. We felt desolate when the other C-47s went their separate ways and our escorts had to break off and return to base.

A couple of hours after leaving the Corridor, we saw a fine-looking airfield directly below us. It appeared that we were coming in to land, but we didn't. It was Kanchow, which the Japanese still imperiled. The plane flew on over the edge of a thick undercast. We passengers didn't know about it until later, but somewhere out over the valley the fuel pump on the port engine had given out. The crew had been able to maintain fuel pressure with the hand-operated wobble pump. After forty-five minutes, the wobble pump was showing signs of distress. The crew chief came aft, opened the cargo door, and said, "All right, fellows, stand by to jump."

Faced with the alternative of riding that overloaded, underpowered, flying gas tank into a crash landing, the prospect of a parachute jump seemed positively alluring: Just crouch on the sill of the cargo door frame and roll out into the nice, cool breeze. We made last minute shuffles of the many things in our escape vests. We knew that the more items we carried, the harder we would hit, but we didn't know when, if ever again, we would find goodies like some of that stuff.

The medical officer smiled blandly and said, "We aren't really going to jump, are we, when we are flying along so nicely?"

At that moment the wobble pump went out and the port engine gave its last gasp. Our one good engine did its best, but there was no way it could keep that heavy load hung up in the sky. The pilot spotted a hole in the undercast and dove for it. I don't know what our airspeed was in that dive, but the wind screamed by like it does through the wires of an open biplane. Nobody could have survived a jump from that crazy, diving aircraft. He would have been blown straight into the horizontal tail. Later, I heard about the rate of climb indicator showing four thousand feet per minute down. The pilot recovered from his dive and visibility was good under the cloud deck. We could see our strip ten miles ahead. But we were out of altitude—we no longer had enough to give us a chance of a survivable jump. I figured that the pilot could belly into some of that rice-paddy country with a survivable landing. We got behind the mail and clung to the cargo tie-down rings.

There was one thing that I had not factored into my figuring. The pilot very neatly traded off speed for distance, and we plunked down on the near end of the strip at Changting with perhaps twenty feet to spare. The Chinese immediately rolled our C-47 to one side and started camouflaging it with freshly cut pine branches. It was the first airplane ever to remain overnight at Changting.

I didn't exactly jump out and kiss the ground, but that ground did feel mighty comforting under the soles of my feet.

The medical officer grinned, but this time his grin was just a little bit sickish.

Chief Storekeeper C. J. King, USNR, met the flight, took the $80,000,000 CN off my hands, and signed the ten receipts. He was one of the finest; a petty officer filling a commissioned officer's billet.

The supply officer in Kunming had been right—the shipment of guard mail hadn't been any trouble for me.

4

CHANGTING

THEN ON TO

NANPING

Perhaps the first thing that newcomers to Fukien Province became aware of was the magnificent and often spectacular scenery. The rainfall was plentiful and most places were green even though much of the countryside had been stripped of its timber long ago. Some reforestation was being practiced. Streams started from springs high in the mountains and spilled down a thousand feet. The land rose up four or five thousand feet and then dropped off into the next valley, with very little tableland between ranges.

We found Changting, Fukien Province, to be a picturesque small town on the Ting Kiang. The airstrip there ran straight into a mountain. Transports landed approaching the mountain and took off headed away from it—never mind the wind direction. The surrounding mountainous, green countryside and the clear stream were indeed beautiful. On several occasions we engaged in prolonged mountain climbing expeditions. The exercise was intended to strengthen our leg muscles for the long hikes coming up.

Changting Air Force Base was somewhat austere by Stateside standards. It had no facilities for dispensing gasoline or oil. Changting radio could work Kunming nine hundred miles to the west, but it couldn't communicate with airplanes directly overhead. Defense equipment consisted of an air raid siren plus one fifty-caliber machine gun which could send tracers through the night in beautiful curving trajectories. No jacks or other ground handling equipment were available, and if an airplane were to taxi off the strip or off its hardstand, it became scrap right then.

Late in the war, a giant four engine B-24, of all things, landed at Changting. The next morning a motor mechanic went out to preflight the engines and turn the B-24 around so that it headed away from the mountain. He let the landing gear on one side get off the broken-up stone and it sank into the mud. The base commander said, "OK, boys, have at it," and everyone there went out to salvage nuts, bolts, tubing and fittings to keep his Jeep running a while longer. A Chinese mechanic cut stainless steel sheets out of the fire walls behind the engines and made watch bands, one of which I still wear. The Americans were learning from the Chinese—let nothing go to waste.

One night a B-25 bomber landed first and acted as a control tower for a half dozen C-46 transports which came in and landed. They unloaded fifty-five gallon drums of aviation gasoline and headed back west. Then a squadron of P-51 fighters, the 75th, landed and parked in a row along the strip. Nothing remotely like this had ever happened at Changting before.

One P-51 was still in the air. As could be seen from the ground, it had a hole at least two feet in diameter through its right wing. It had been on a fighter sweep over Hong Kong and had taken an ack-ack hit. The pilot had elected to join up with the 75th and fly into Changting rather than attempt to fly all the way back to Chihkiang with his own squadron. For about twenty minutes he circled the strip teaching himself how to fly a Mustang with a big hole in its wing. I looked away briefly. When I looked back into the sky I couldn't find him. I asked the person next to me, "Where is the P-51?"

He pointed to a column of smoke starting to rise from a point well outside the field. The pilot had tried lowering his gear and flaps and this had thrown the crippled airplane into an uncontrollable dive. He had been a squadron commander and those who knew him said that he was particularly fine. Ironically, for quite a while, he could have jumped with virtually no risk.

See CHANGTING!

Beauty Spot of Southeast China

We Recommend THE CHUNG NAN HOTEL
W. F. BULL, Prop.

* *

Rooms Available Day or Night

———

Cuisine Supreme in the Namyung Room
M. LE ROUGE RYKE, Maitre d'Hotel

———

East China's Only Transportation
and Communication Center
For The West

———

Free or Fast Laundry

———

Two Direct Lines to Heaven:
(1) Padre J. COSGROVE, Official Service
(2) 10th WX, Faster But Not Too Reliable

The NAMYUNG ROOM FEATURES

* *

Southern Fried Chicken
a la HIGHTOWER

———

Strawberry Shortcake

———

ICE COLD Lemonade (Courtesy of Doc ESPEY)

———

Prompt and Attentive Service
At All Times

———

Two Sweets for Birthdays
(Only One Birthday per Month)

———

Clean T-Shirts are *de Rigueur*
(Unless We Have Visiting Brass)

ACTIVITIES AT THE CHUNG NAN

* *

Boating	Chess
Swimming	Ping Pong
Hunting	Cards

Fishing (Pistols or Plastic only)

Dancing	Concerts

Moonlight *Ching-Paos*

———

Intra-Service Sport Competitions

———

Sack Time Logging (Most Popular)

———

Under Competent Direction of
Padre J. COSGROVE
Dispenser of T. S. Cards

Changting Also Offers:

* *

Side Trips to Foochow, Nanping, Yungan,
and All Points East

___

Accommodation for Navy, Marines, OSS, TAI,
AGAS (What the Hell, They're Our Allies)

___

Wine, Women, Song, and Honey Buckets

___

Stories of Janaski's Stateside Toilet ——
But Good!

___

Supply Point for Souvenirs:

Lacquer	Silver
Fans	Carvings
Seals	Engraving

___

Have You Eaten at Red's Snack Bar?

Have You Heard About Our Boys
on the Fox Hole Front in East China?

* *

Surrounded by the Deadly Jap?

___

Hundreds of Kilos Behind the Lines?

___

The Rice and Cucumber Diet?

___

Slaving 16 and 18 Hours Per Day?

___

Well, THIS IS IT !

___

COME TO CHANGTING!!
IT'S ROUGH, — BUT GOOD!!!

___

Approved:

The Hack	J. B. Head
Nbr, 2 Boy	AACS

A pamphlet that some of the men put together to give "tourists."

A few of the other fighters sustained superficial damage. A couple of them were damaged too much to go on a sweep over Shanghai, but the rest of the squadron took off on schedule. Replacement parts were flown in from Kunming and the badly damaged fighters were salvaged.[1]

That night dissident Chinese built bonfires aligned with the strip some distance from each end. One Japanese bomber came over, lined up with the bonfires, set its intervalometer, and dropped a string of bombs along the entire length of the strip. Then it flew back to Kanchow, loaded one blockbuster of a bomb, and came back and tried to crater the strip, but succeeded only in excavating a huge pit right next to it.

To repair the bomb damage, the Chinese had coolies bring in fill dirt in baskets on the ends of their yoyo poles. They dragged a large tree stump into the hole. This stump had one hundred lines radiating from it in all directions. They stationed coolies around the brink of the hole, one at the end of each line. An old character with a loud, high-pitched voice sang a song with innumerable verses. One note in each verse was accented, and with that note each coolie would exert an all-out pull on his line. The stump would rise a foot or so and then thump down, compacting the fill dirt under it. By sunset, the hole was filled up to grade with firm material.

The commanding officer there was a peppery little, old, army retread, Major W. F. Bull, USA, who sported around the area on a high-powered motorcycle. The chaplain was a universally liked Catholic priest, Father J. Cosgrove, who conducted both Catholic and Protestant services. Father Cosgrove, known as the "Pistol-Packing Padre," was not always a winner. There came a time when the base cat was obviously going to have kittens. The padre was moved to wager the base commander that the cat would not have more than five. The day of the big event arrived with much fanfare. As each kitten dropped, a communique would be issued, rapidly permeating to every corner of the base. Finally the announcement came, "Five dropped, more coming." The padre solemnly walked over and said to the CO, "Sir, here is your $500 CN." It wasn't even close—the final tally was nine. And out there a kitten would bring $25 gold, what with the rats and all.

A small mess hall was built at Changting. During the summer it got hot and airless in there. Fortunately the room had a high ceiling, so the houseboys made a large rectangular frame and stretched fabric across it. They hinged the upper edge to the overhead and ran lines from the lower edge in both directions. Houseboys were stationed at the ends of the lines. First one of them would pull on his line, and then the other. The big sheet, known as a *"punkah,"* stirred up a very welcome movement of air in the room. Those who pulled the lines were *"punkah wallahs."* It was straight out of Rudyard Kipling.

The fellows at Changting, after I had been there a short while, said that three professors there who had been evacuated from Foochow loved to play bridge but couldn't find a fourth. Well, now . . . a friend and I had participated in weekly duplicate bridge tournaments for several years. I made a date with those professors. By the end of the second hand it was obvious that their bridge was on so much higher a plane than mine that we decided to devote the rest of the evening to polite conversation.

In the old days, I heard, Christian missionaries in Changting had tried to keep enough rice on hand so that they could feed a little to any hungry convert who showed up. Cynics claimed that the only reason the converts came was to get the rice. The term "Rice Christian" became very prevalent.

Some Buddhist monks maintained a temple on top of a little mountain that rose about five hundred feet above the plain. The temple contained several rows of statues, all in surprisingly good condition. I suppose that the rather strenuous climb up the mountain had dissuaded typical lowlife marauders from vandalizing the place. Each idol had a different theme. The most popular stood for fertility, and local women always left a good supply of little gifts in front of it.

I visited the temple quite frequently during the time I was waiting for my colleagues to jeep down from Nanping and pick us up. The monks served absolutely delicious little ricecakes and tea. The cynics undoubtedly would have said that I was only a "Ricecake Buddhist."

I was billeted in the tallest building in Changting (four stories), so when the *jing bao* (air raid alarm) sounded, I usually thought it advisable to walk out into the countryside. One time, a young Chinese accompanied me. We found good cover, which we never needed. While we were waiting for the all clear, some animal, quite close by, made an amazingly loud noise. I asked, "What was that?"

My friend said, "My English is very limited. I do not know the English word for the animal. However, it has four legs and is good to eat."

I suggested, "Water buffalo?"

He laughed and said no. When we got back to town he looked up another Chinese who had a firmer command of the English language and asked him to tell me the name of the loud animal.

The second Chinese said, "Bullfrog."

One day soon afterwards, James J. Janasky, Captain USA, and Delbert J. Burton, ACMM USNR, veteran TAI field personnel, drove a Jeep down from Nanping to pick us up in Changting. The following day we jounced northward over the wild, one-lane road which wound its way through the mountains; one stretch covered a hundred and sixty-five kilometers without a single fork or crossing. This road was the lifeline of the area in which we were to be stationed.

We stopped for the night at Yungan, halfway to Nanping, and put up at the Office of War Information hostel there, an establishment run by Christopher Rand, a well-known author who wrote learned articles for the *New Yorker Magazine*. We saw a lot more of his assistant, an ex-pugilist known as The Turnip. This character had prepared for us by laying in an ample stock of *bei kan jiu*, the local rice brandy. He mixed it with something or other in a beautiful large cut glass bowl, but the mixer failed to take the curse off the brandy.

The Turnip had a young goat named Rudolph. He said, "In a few weeks Rudolph is going to be tethered out in the jungle for a tiger hunt."

One of the party was an OSS agent whom I had come to know pretty well. He carried a personal accurized M1903 Army Springfield rifle. When it got dark, he drew a bead on a streetlight way over on the far side of town. I held a cigarette lighter so as to illuminate his front sight. One round took care of the streetlight. The mayor of Yungan pulled a *jing bao* so that he could turn off the rest of his street lights without losing face.

The party lasted quite a few hours and got quite maudlin. Finally everyone had had enough. Turnip dashed the cut-glass bowl to the floor. Then he attacked a nice, rattan sofa occupying the middle of the room, kicked it into splinters, and threw the wreckage out-of-doors. This provided room for everyone to stretch out on the floor in their sleeping bags. Turnip then ended the party by extinguishing the overhead light with a couple of rounds from his .45.

I came to. It was daylight. I rolled over and heard the loud crunching noise of broken glass. I opened my eyes and saw that three of us were lying in the middle of a ring of black cloth shoes. The Chinese in the establishment, politely ignoring the Americans on the floor, were partaking of their breakfast as usual.

I soon realized that I had the granddaddy of all hangovers. The OSS man was even worse off. Rudolph the goat had crapped in his custom-made boots and he didn't know it until he put them on. Rudolph's career very nearly reached its finale before he ever had a chance to play a leading role in a tiger hunt.

The Turnip's path and mine crossed several times after that, but never again did I set out partying with him.

Janasky, Burton and I finally dragged into Nanping and parked in the lot next to the hotel. Janasky removed the battery from our Jeep and had it lugged up to our base by a couple of coolies, to confound the hot-wire artists.

Nanping was at the confluence of the Kien Kiang and the Sha Kiang, which together formed the Min Kiang, flowing southeasterly to Foochow and the sea. The town was on a flat area a little above river water level, ringed by mountains.[2] The geographical center of the entire Japanese Empire was very close to Nanping when we arrived there.

First Lieutenant Russel D. Martinko, USA, was being rotated out of China after a term of distinguished service, and turned his Jeep over to me, along with detailed instructions on how to keep it running under austere conditions. He gave me maps, marked to show which roads were still passable, priceless information on places to stay in the territory, and whom to contact at each—military, civilian, missionary, Chinese, whatever. His help was invaluable and freely given.

Our commanding officer, Major Slack, remained in Kunming during this time. He had tried to visit our unit in the middle of the preceding winter, but the C-47 he was on got lost in a snow storm and ran out of gas. Everybody aboard bailed out successfully but they had a mighty rugged time getting back to base. He did not try to visit the unit again until the following summer, but he did everything he could to get us equipment and personnel. He did not try in any way to control our operations. This was just as well, since we were a rambunctious crew twelve hundred miles away with no radio of our own.

We invariably called each other by our surnames. We never saluted and never referred to rank or rating. We all ate and slept in the same places. Of course, the officers made the decisions and told the others what to do.

We never wore uniforms out there. Too conspicuous. Janasky wore his two bars showing that he was a captain. Under the Geneva Convention this meant that he should be treated with some respect if he were captured. But since when did the Japanese (or many of our people either) pay any attention to the Convention? I decided that I would be less likely to get caught if I didn't wear any insignia denoting rank.

I was frankly somewhat surprised that BuPers (Bureau of Naval Personnel) had allowed me to have duty in occupied territory. The two years I had just served in Washington had loaded me with sensitive information. Perhaps those desk pilots there did not realize that the day was long past when a prisoner of war, no matter how resolute, could hold out against an enemy interrogation team. The understanding was: Carry as much ammo as you can. If you are surrounded and escape is impossible, take as many of them with you as you can. But save the last cartridge for yourself. Have the bullet for this cartridge made of silver in your honor. Or pretend that you are going to.

Would I have used the "silver bullet"? I do not know. The occasion never arose. I think that I would have.

The view from the front yard of the Downey House was spectacular.
(Photo by Bellew)

Our unit's base in Nanping had been a Methodist medical missionary's home. The mission occupied a walled compound that circled around much of the town. At the far end of the compound was some kind of a navy post run by a petty officer named Lucas, who was an Old China Hand. Lucas was the spokesman for all of us in any dealings with the local Chinese. At our end of the compound was a school for girls of about fifteen. It was the only Methodist activity left.

An old missionary gentleman, whom I can only describe as being pretty much of a milquetoast, was in charge. His assistant was a gaunt, old Australian gal of great character named Miss Wallace. We military types irreverently spoke of her as Pruneface.

Another of our neighbors was the British Consulate, which had been evacuated from Foochow. I never did know what all of the other units in the compound were. A Chinese Army garrison nearby had a bugler whose weird call woke us up every morning. He seemed to elide his notes.

The view from our front yard over the trees to the confluence of the rivers was magnificent. Nanping had electric lights, an excellent shopping street, and even a commercial ice plant. All in all, it was by far the finest town in Southeast China.

----

[1] Changing time frames, the 1989 movie, "Empire of the Sun," showed how a P-51 sweep on Shanghai looked to the people on the ground. It brought back to me vivid memories of the time I saw a fighter sweep on Shanghai being staged through Changting.

[2] By 1988 Nanping, now on the railroad, was a thriving lumber town with a population of 160,000.

TAI's comfortable quarters in Nanping, the Downey House. (Photo by Bellew)

Burton, Featherstone, Peppler, Janasky (in a Japanese parachute), Millard, Corbin, Winborn at Downey House. (Photo by interpreter)

The commanding officer, Major Slack, visits TAI unit, Nanping, July 1945. Rear row, left to right: Orville E. Millard, ACMM, USNR; James L. Brown, S/Sgt. AUG; Byron R. Winborn, Lt., USNR; Morris W. Slack, Maj., AUS; John R. Peppler, Ens., USNR; Delbert J. Burton, ACMM, USNR.
Front row, left to right: Norman B. Oppenheimer, S/Sgt., AUS; George T. Yamamura, S/Sgt., AUS; Harold R. Featherstone, Cpl., AUS; Donald R. Bellew, PhoM 1c, USNR. (Photo by interpreter)

5

Learning

to Know

the Territory

Japan was the predominant surface power in China, with garrisons in many towns. Its troop could go just about anywhere they wanted to, although sometimes against resistance. But except when they were making a drive, they were disinclined to venture forth into the unfriendly countryside.

The Japanese maintained a garrison in each major port along the Southeast China coast, and, shadowing the garrison, would be a Sino-American Cooperative Organization (SACO) camp back in the hills. Chinese guerrillas, trained at these camps, inflicted severe punishment on the coastal garrisons, and the Americans participated in some of the firefights. SACO generated a wealth of intelligence. An elaborate coast watcher organization reported on enemy shipping movements up and down the coast, which furnished rich targets for Fourteenth Air Force bombing runs. The major weather systems in the area moved from west to east, so that data on the weather in China was invaluable to the US Fleet out there in the Pacific.

SACO ran a hospital for Chinese casualties, outposts here and there in the eastern part of my territory, and operated in other parts of China.

Why wasn't most of this an army mission? Because the army knew next to nothing about how to operate in China. But the navy, through years of experience with the Yangtze River Patrol, had acquired familiarity with Chinese customs, traditions, and culture and had powerful political contacts, notably General Tai Li, the sometimes dreaded head of the secret police.

SACO's political contacts with the Chinese Nationalist Government were ultra right wing, whereas the Fourteenth Air Force's contacts were decidedly pink. The Air Force part of my organization preferred that I have as little contact as possible with SACO units. I was not responsive to such suggestions, particularly since I drew my pay from a disbursing officer at SACO's establishment in Kienyang, a four-hour drive north of Nanping. I stopped over in SACO camps and outposts whenever convenient.

The fellows in SACO composed a song about life in China, a typical verse of which was:

"I thought I got the word at the ICB
But there ain't no room in the honey pot
For the crap they handed me."

SACO, of course, included Marine personnel.

AGAS—Air-Ground Aid Service—drew its authority directly from the White House, having the function of getting downed American airmen safely back to rear areas. It was composed of air force, navy and civilian personnel. You may guess how AGAS was pronounced.

AGFRTS was an acronym for Air-Ground Forces Resources Technical Staff. All kinds of devices were used to make American intelligence operations more palatable to our host ally. This particular venture was part of Colonel "Wild Bill" Donovan's Office of Strategic Services. OSS was the forerunner of the CIA. The pronunciation of AGFRTS was also obvious.

Service with TAI in Southeast China was construed to be "hazardous duty behind enemy lines" which brought navy personnel a handsome per diem. This amused us because we could live as high on the hog as was possible out there and still not spend $20 gold a month. Money we had. The Air Force personnel in our unit were awarded bronze medals in lieu of hazardous duty pay.

I looked forward to some stimulating duty.

Years before all these military operations entered China, the Christian missionaries realized that it would be self-defeating to let the various denominations compete against one another out in the provinces where their coverage was spread pathetically thin, so they had agreed to an assignment of regions. All of the southern portion of my territory (including Nanping) was Methodist country. The northern portion was Roman Catholic.

The Methodists planted good gardens. Methodist missions were the only places where it was safe to eat raw vegetables. The Methodists set excellent tables, but they never put out ashtrays, and as for drinking . . . .

The Catholics in Nancheng, Suweng, and their associates in Linchuan, were more haphazard about the chow they served; but some of them, particularly the charming Irish in Nancheng, served surprisingly good wine. One of them liked to say, "The situation in China is hopeless, but not serious." They loved American cigarettes when we could get them. Father Venadam, a French-Canadian in Lungchuan, could offer a good cigar. Three German monks in Kuangtse were the only persons in Southeast China who could give us a glass of milk. They had their own dairy cow.

At first it did seem a little odd to stay at a German mission, but any possible differences between our two countries were confined to another world and had nothing to do with life in China. The Father Superior was supposed to have returned to Germany for one year after serving in China for ten years. He had now been out there eighteen years with still no relief in sight. Conditions in his fatherland had been disturbed.

Along with the missionary situation, travel conditions in China also took some getting used to. Only one passable north-south road, with a few branches, was available to us. It passed right through Nanping. Most places were reachable only by walking, riding sampans, and occasionally, horseback riding. We could rely on the Chinese to keep us informed of any possible approach of a Japanese detachment toward Nanping, and we had an impressive arsenal with rifles, hand grenades, and bazookas to greet them. If a detachment bigger than we cared to take on came around, we would hit the trail for the mountains with full confidence that we could walk faster than they could.

Walking was the most characteristic mode of travel. The distance walked was expressed in *li*, a term also applied to travel by sampan. *Li* was a somewhat imprecise measure. It was perhaps best defined by saying that if one walked briskly and took one ten minute rest period each hour, he would cover an average of ten *li* per hour. Sometimes the number of *li* up to the top of a mountain was considered to be greater than the number for the return trip. A *li* usually worked out to be about one-third of a mile or half a kilometer.

The Chinese loved cobblestone trails one-person wide. Each step would give your ankle a little twist. The trails in Fukien were virtually impassable at night. Even in the daytime, you had to ignore the grand scenery and watch every step you took. The moment you lifted your gaze up to a waterfall, you would step off the trail into a rice paddy, start slipping off the mountainside, or smash your teeth into the pole on the coolie in front of you.

At one location there was a continuous cobblestone staircase zigzagging up the mountain. After climbing for awhile you would start to see blue sky at the end of each zig or zag. But each time the trail would double back again. One day I made the mistake of counting the steps—there were over twenty-seven hundred in one stretch. This by no means got you to the top—only a short distance ahead was another flight of five hundred and sixty steps. Later on we climbed much higher mountains.

Some trails were located on the dikes between rice paddies. Some went up rocky creek beds. The most comfortable were those in mud. It appeared that all the trails had been in their present locations for centuries. No doubt we should have been imbued with thoughts of all the people who had traversed these routes throughout their long history. More often, we were preoccupied with wondering if that sensation in our legs warned of incipient cramps, and whether our rice and eggs that evening would be as delectable as ever.

Coolies were often a source of wonder. The traditional day's work for a professional carrier coolie was to carry eighty catties one hundred *li*. This standard was well-established. The coolie might demand and

Our lifeline, our connection with the outside world, the road from our air strip at
Changting north toward our base at Nanping. One stretch of this wild mountain
road ran one hundred and sixty five kilometers without a sideroad or fork.
(Photo by Winborn)

get $100 CN per ten *li*. "Catty" was the English word for a unit of weight
used only in Eastern Asia. One catty was said to be about one and a third
pounds. A professional coolie started his apprenticeship while he was a
teenager, gradually building up callouses on his shoulders one quarter
inch thick. He learned to move with a loping gait which spared the load
from any jouncing. Few of the coolies we used came up to the standards.

When we were returning from a wreck we might need as many as
four coolies per person in our party. I wanted to be fair to the coolies
that we hired, getting the service that I had paid for without over-
burdening the man. Between trips my interpreter and I went down into
Nanping's main shopping street looking for some catty scales. This item
was basically a wooden beam suspended from a cord located at a fulcrum
on one side of its mid-point. A cord from the short side led to the item
being weighed. A weight would be slid along the long side of the beam

until the scales balanced. The position of the sliding weight indicated in catties the weight of the object.

We located a likely-looking merchant and asked, "Do you have any catty scales?"

The merchant said, "Good, good, good. Do you want buying scales or selling scales?"

"We want correct scales."

"Surely you must be either buying or selling."

I never did find out whether the scales he sold us were for buying or selling.

All citizens had either to pay a heavy tax or to volunteer their services to the magistrate one day out of every twenty. Sometimes a magistrate would furnish these people to us as carrier coolies. They would not have the calloused shoulder of a professional, and the results were often pathetic. The magistrate would pay each one $100 CN plus three catties of rice per day. This was a two-day supply of rice, but, after all, they had to walk back again the next day.

Sometimes I would think that I was getting pretty good, having just hiked ninety *li* carrying my automatic and a light sheath knife. Then I would notice that a small coolie girl had loped along in front of me all day toting sixty catties of my gear on her shoulder. Did she feel resentment toward me? Oh, no. Typically she would appear to be quite philosophical about her role in the world during this reincarnation, feeling only admiration for the large American because he was above having to carry a burden on his shoulder.

In some areas, the women were the better carriers. At the start of a day a man might find that his assigned load was on the heavy side, so he would turn it over to his wife and look for something lighter. In the next area, the women might be next to worthless for getting any work done.

We tried to be kind to our volunteers and generally paid them even though we didn't have to. Once our coolies refused to accept any pay, saying that they wanted to contribute to the war effort. Once.

One day we had particularly poor coolies. They malingered all the way. When we ordered them to speed up, they moaned about being too tired to go any faster. Then, late in the day, they put on a burst of speed and loped off the last ten *li* in only forty-five minutes. As we paid them off, we asked, "How do you manage to go so fast after you have been dragging along all day?"

The answer was typically Chinese. "It is getting dark."

Another frequent mode of travel was by sampan on the rivers. This obviated the hassle of getting coolies, and even though we were accomplished walkers, getting there by sampan held a definite appeal. If we were to continue by sampan the next day, we would stretch out on the deck and sleep aboard. A small clay fireplace in the stern, with a wok, was provided for cooking our meals. The gunwales afforded us our sanitary facilities. River water became drinking water after boiling, although sometimes a boatman would dip a cup into the river, quench his thirst and politely offer the cup to us.

To propel a large three-man sampan, one boatman would go way forward, face aft, stick his pole into the river bottom, lean on it, and walk along one side of the deck until he reached the stern. Another boatman would walk the other side of the sampan. The third boatman would steer, and the three of them would take turns. In a smaller two-man sampan, one boatman would take up a station in the bow and the other at the stern. Both would push on their poles without walking.

The sampans were constructed of rather wide wooden boards with what appeared to be a tung oil finish. They had canopies of woven split bamboo. With good lines, they were stable and durable. Most of the rivers were placid, but occasionally we would get a ride down whitewater rapids. The helmsmen had great skill at such ventures, and often showed what struck us as real courage.

Sampaning was not a rapid mode of travel, but the boatmen worked long hours and would cover a good distance in a day, leaving us with enough energy to forge onward the following day.

One day I "joined the cavalry"—rented a horse—to rest my legs. Horses in China were very small, often called "Mongolian ponies." Each horse was accompanied by his groom who walked or trotted alongside all the way holding on to the bridle. The saddle was wood and cloth; the reins were clothesline. With the stirrups set as low as they would go, my knees were above the horse's back. I wore out one nag in eighteen *li* and

"Just patch the bad spot and it will work fine." (Photo by Mattmiller)

Sampans along the Min Kiang at a tributary. (Photo by Bellew)

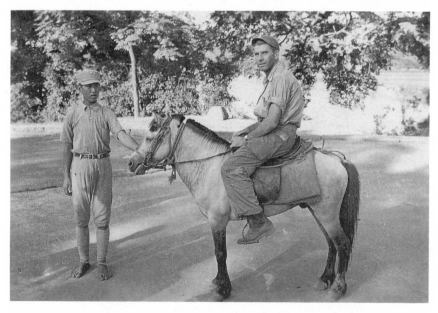

Millard on horseback at Kanchow. (Photo by Janasky)

then was given a really rugged little beast who was always ready to run. His gallop was not too uncomfortable. But when he came back down to a trot he went through a vibration period that really rattled my teeth. We left the "infantry" far behind that day.

We rented horses on numerous other occasions. This provided welcome relief for our legs, somewhat at the expense of other portions of our anatomies.

Except for what the coolies carried on their yoyo poles or sampans carried on the rivers and canals, all freight and passenger traffic was handled by a fleet of prewar trucks, some Daimler-Benz, but mostly Dodge. As the years went by, they were gradually assimilated into China by some sort of intermarriage such as had been the case with the foreign hordes who had conquered China from time to time.

Passengers and cargo shared the bed of the truck, which was covered with a woven split bamboo canopy. The crew of four sat in a row on the bench in the cab. The mechanic sat on the left. Next came the driver. Then the woman who did the cooking and the laundry. Finally, and most important, the man who handled what airplane people would call a "chock," which was triangular and had handles like a rolling pin. As a truck bogged down going up a mountain, this man would jump out and, with exquisite timing, jam his chock under a rear wheel at the precise moment forward motion ceased. Part of the cargo would be off-loaded so the truck could proceed up the hill.

It was rumored that these trucks had had brakes when they were purchased from Dodge.

Not infrequently, a truck would break down in the middle of a one-lane road. If a connecting rod bearing burned out, the mechanic would meticulously fashion pieces of bamboo to replace the babbitt. Bamboo is apparently a fine anti-friction material. Pretty soon the mechanic would have neat little rows of engine parts laid out all over the place. It could be extremely difficult to drive a Jeep around a truck broken down in the mountains.

Most surprisingly, after a couple of days a broken-down truck would always start up and the crew would resume its journey.

Twenty-six gallons of gasoline had to leave Calcutta to put one gallon down on the strip at Changting. So forget about having any for running Jeeps and trucks!

Fortunately, our Jeeps would run well on a fuel called "pine gas" that the Chinese distilled from the roots and stumps of pine trees in the southern half of my territory. A delightful piney aroma would be left behind when a Jeep using it drove past. Just about full power would be developed and there was no knocking.

Pine gas had one major shortcoming—a very high flash point. To start a cold engine, you had to dip a rag into the gas tank under the seat, wrap it around the carburetor, and light it with a match. Red flames fringed with black smoke shot up into the air. The moment the flames died down, you could hit the starter button and it would take right off. No problem. A hot engine would re-start for as much as twenty seconds without needing another bonfire around the carburetor. In the northern half of my territory, we could buy ethyl alcohol distilled from fermented rice. Not being clarified in any way, it stank to high heaven with a vomit-like odor. Starting involved no heroic measures and there was no knocking. But before your engine would run on alcohol you had to take the carburetor all apart, remove the jet and replace it with a drilled-out jet having a much larger orifice. Of course, you had to reverse this procedure to convert back to pine gas.

There was nothing insurmountable about changing jets, but it was a time-consuming chore that just might have to be performed during a heavy rain. So, once between trips I got a little part from a Japanese airplane and had the local machinist make it into a small needle valve. This artisan ran a one-man piston factory. Well, he did have one boy to power his lineshaft by turning a crank. The factory was a bamboo shanty which backed up to a steep hill that acted as its rear wall. It had a forge used for blacksmith work, melting aluminum, and cooking dinner. He melted up aluminum skin from Japanese airplanes and cast and machined pistons for the pre-war Dodge trucks in the area. I have never encountered a machinist in the States who had mastered all of the skills this one had. Anyway, I mounted my new needle valve in a little piece of copper tubing and soldered the tube into holes I had drilled in the carburetor

A jeep, a road sign and Bellew near Nanping. (Photo by Winborn)

body, by-passing the jet (the material would solder). Presto! In pine gas country the carburetor was just right with the needle valve closed, in rice alcohol country just right with it open. Changing over took only seconds.

Not long after I started using my new by-pass, I lit off a pine gas start. This melted the solder and the valve plinked out onto the ground. I had to devise a way of clamping everything in place. When I was very lucky, I might have gained possession of a bottle partly full of some chemical or other, always odorous, and sometimes stinking, which, when dribbled into the carburetor would act as a primer gas for starting.

Pine gas would quickly dissolve the material used for the diaphragms in Jeep fuel pumps. Some nameless genius had found that dried Chinese pig's bladder fulfilled this function perfectly. I always carried a spare pig's bladder under the seat. The diaphragm proved to be so durable that I never had to replace it.

Some of the old Dodge trucks had water gas generators installed on the side to provide fuel.

Truly, we fought a high tech war out there in Southeast China, where the people were fortunate to have such a highly developed transportation system.

Whatever we traveled on or in, highway bridges were virtually unknown and rivers had to be crossed by ferry. Some of my colleagues once arrived at a ferry and found the crew gone, so they decided to pole the barge across themselves. The result was that they lost control and drifted downstream nine *li* before they could come to a stop. They had to hire fifty coolies to drag the barge back to its usual mooring place. (See p. 98 in Chapter 8 for a photograph.)

On another afternoon's drive we encountered four ferries, all poled by hand. It was almost dark when we arrived at the last one. The barge was tied up across the river with a charcoal burning truck aboard it, ready to embark. The truck refused to start. Another truck had been waiting on our side for hours. We surveyed the situation and found that a second barge, slightly smaller, was tied up on our side of the river.

I said, "Take us across on the smaller barge."

"Yes, yes. But there is only one landing on the far side."

"Move the barge at the landing ten meters upstream and tie it up. That truck on it isn't going to start today anyway."

"That is possible, but there are no poles on this side."

"Well, send a man across that footbridge fifty meters upstream and have some poles brought over here."

"Yes, yes. Can do."

I then asked, "Shouldn't the truck that has waited on this side for so long go first?"

"Oh, no. The military always goes first."

But, of course.

Did the Japanese keep track of where we were when we were on trips? We were to find the answer to this was affirmative.

6

THE TRAINING TRIP

AND

PIRATES' BAY TRIP

"A Japanese plane is down!" exclaimed one of our Chinese interpreters, reading the local newspaper a few days after our arrival in Nanping. Supposedly when an enemy plane came down, the local Chinese authorities would send word up the monolithic governmental organization to the capital in Chungking, which would pass the word to the Fourteenth Air Force Headquarters in Kunming, who would tell the TAI unit there. TAI in Kunming would then notify whichever of its field units was closest to the crash site. Our interpreter had bypassed the system.

"Good," said Janasky. "Just the right time to take Winborn and Millard out on a training trip. The village where the airplane landed is southeast of here. We can take the overnight steamboat downriver to Mintsing, which is as close to the Japanese garrison as the boats dare go. At Mintsing the Americans get off and start walking and the Chinese board sampans for the rest of the trip to Foochow."

Each vessel of the Min River Steamboat Company, like some of the old Dodge trucks around China, actually had an internal combustion engine fueled with water gas, which was produced in an on-board gas generator. This contraption was a vertical steel cylinder in which air flowed upward through a deep bed of glowing charcoal over a grate. A tin can with nail holes in the bottom was used to drip water onto the fire. The addition of water droplets generated hydrogen plus carbon monoxide. Any carbon dioxide formed was reduced to carbon monoxide in the upper layers of the fuel bed. Water gas, then, was largely a mixture of nitrogen, hydrogen and carbon monoxide, which when added to air and drawn into the engine by its suction, would burn and produce power. There must have been many other compounds present in the water gas because the exhaust had a distinctive chemical sort of odor. A handblower was used to operate the generator until the engine started and its suction took over. The engine drove a propeller.

These vessels were sizable, some ninety feet long with fourteen staterooms. Each stateroom was cubical, five feet six inches in each direction, with bunks for four persons. I absentmindedly stretched out on my bunk and pushed my boots through the window between the stateroom and the corridor down the center of the ship. The Chinese thought it uproariously amusing that the American was so tall—five feet, ten inches.

The latrine was a stool on an outrigger jutting out from the stern of the ship. It could be a mighty lonely place on a dark night with the rest of the ship up ahead and the water swirling below.

We left our steamboat at Mintsing, got coolies to carry our gear, and started the four-day walk to the village where the plane was down.

TAI is an organization of many tales—mostly right good yarns even before the embroidery is added. One of the classics is the sad story of the Focke-Wulf 190 and the bomb disposal officer. This FW-190, fresh from Italy, was received in the hangar at Anacostia in flyable condition. The TAI experts scrutinized every detail. It became obvious that the canopy was fitted with an explosive release. Thus, when the urge to bail out came upon the pilot, he could push a button and, "Boom!" the canopy would sail off into space and the pilot was cleared for immediate departure. Now it so happened that (except in China) bombs, booby traps, and other fiendish explosive devices were not routinely handled by TAI. Instead, the TAI officer called in the nearest bomb disposal officer and exchanged pleasantries with him, indicating that "Bomb disposal officers are expendable—we're not!"

Anyway, a young bomb disposal officer with the rank of Lieutenant, Junior Grade, was called along with his assistant to the hangar at

Anacostia to deactivate the explosive canopy-release on the FW-190. The base commander, and other important gold braid, gathered around because the FW-190 was a very hot item in those days. The various "Verboten" decals were translated for the bomb disposal officer, and he began tracing out circuits with that deft touch which only comes from great experience. "Connect this wire," he barked to the assistant.

"Kapow!" With a report that shook the hangar, the canopy shot aft carrying away the vertical fin and rudder, continuing along a trajectory that barely missed the assembled braid. It crashed to the deck at the far end of the hangar, a mangled monument to the effectiveness of German ordnance and an awful smear upon the reputation of the bomb disposal people.

Naval Group China was an organization with a penchant for setting up outposts in remote spots where the idea of finding navy would seem too ludicrous for words. Yungtai was such a spot. As you may have forgotten, Yungtai is located between Lutu and Wotungwel. If that doesn't help, I can only say that it is hidden away in the mountains behind Foochow, which is a very proper place for it to be.

The navy maintained two outposts in Yungtai. The skipper of the newer one was a young JG. One evening during our training trip we slogged into his establishment, definitely the worse for wear after the infamous ninety *li* trudge over "Crying Mountain." After chow-down, the conversation turned to many things and I trotted out the TAI story about the FW-190, just to amuse the lonely JG. He laughed, a little lamely it seemed.

"I must confess," he finally said. "I was the bomb disposal officer who blew the canopy off that FW-190. I have come more than halfway around the world in an attempt to live down the affair. And now it has caught up to me again—even in Yungtai."

There was no further hope.

We found that first downed airplane in very poor condition, but, of course, we could identify it. It was a Nate—a vintage army plane with fixed landing gear. It had very little intelligence significance other than to demonstrate that the Japanese were being forced to use obsolete equipment to carry on their war in China. Given this situation, some Japanese in China guessed that Japan was not going to win and they began to act more amenable to everyone. Others remained unreconstructed.

We heard about one Japanese pilot from people in the vicinity. He had gotten lost and had landed skillfully in a tight space. Usually the Chinese killed an enemy flyer as soon as his plane stopped rolling, but this time they simply formed a circle around him some hundred feet away. The pilot got out. He spat on the ground to indicate his disgust for all things Chinese. He smoked a cigarette and opened the fuel drain cock, letting the gas run out. He then unhooked a hand grenade from his belt, armed it, and tossed it into the cockpit. The explosion blew things apart and started a big fire, into which he jumped, drew out a knife, and committed hara-kiri. Thus ended the life of one unreconstructed Japanese.

On the other hand, a major in the Japanese garrison at Foochow had concluded that Japan was not going to win this war and that there was no future in being a Japanese officer. He bought a ticket on the Min River Steamboat line and cruised upriver to Nanping, where he checked in at the local hotel, which incidentally was much better than average. He toured Nanping's impressive shopping district, all in full uniform. No Americans happened to be on the street that day. Then he walked over to the stockade where the local Chinese troops were garrisoned. He approached the young sentry at the gate, saying, "Request permission to visit the commanding general." The sentry said, "No. You Jap. You bad. You can't come in here." The major, much the sturdier of the two, slugged the youth, knocking him out cold. He then proceeded into the general's office and said, "Sir, I commit myself to your custody." Janasky's comment on the incident was, "You never know what is going to happen next, but it always does."

While we were working over the data we got from our obsolete wreck, a navy type showed up and told us that another airplane had just come down on the coast, only two or three days' walk from where we were. We set out immediately for the site. We had prospects of analyzing two airplanes on one trip!

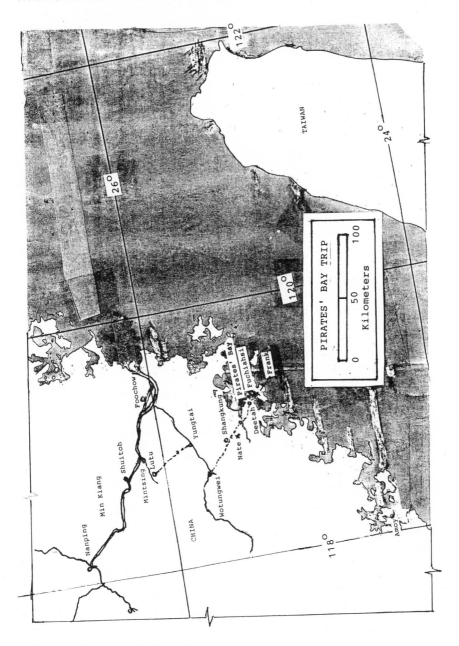

Trip to Pirates' Bay
(Map by Winborn)

On our way to the coast, we stopped over in one side of the police station at Deetah. It was dark in there so we went down the street and bought a few lamps and some peanut oil. To fry our eggs that night we drained a couple of lamps into the wok. After the eggs were fried, we poured the oil back into the lamps.

The latrine in Deetah was prominently located in what would be called *el centro* in a Mexican village. It was an elaborate six-holer, three on each side of a central partition. It had a roof, but no side-walls. I occupied one of the holes for its intended purpose. A friendly local woman came in and took over the next hole, chatting volubly in *Putien-hua*, the local dialect. I couldn't understand a word, but this dialect was easy to identify by its "shlay-shluss" sounds.

A patrol of guerrilla soldiers, trained by the navy, took over the other side of the police station. One of them complained of severe abdominal pains. Appendicitis? We did what we could. We gave him an aspirin tablet and chipped in enough money to buy him a litter ride back to the city the next day.

Around midnight the rest of the soldiers went out on a mission. In about fifteen minutes we heard rifle fire. In another twenty minutes they were back. They had knocked over an enemy radio station operated by five people. One was a woman. They got her in the butt just as she was crawling over the compound wall. The raid had been a success. The patrol had taken no casualties. All five of the enemy were dead.

The next morning our two parties went their separate ways. The raid was now history. The appendicitis patient felt just fine. Aspirin is truly a miracle drug.

We found that the second airplane was a Frank, one of the latest models. We spent three days working it over and accumulating a wealth of prime intelligence. The pilot had made an expert wheels-up landing on a sandy beach with a very gradual slope, and, aside from a bent propeller, damage was slight.

The tide must have been thirty feet there in the Straits of Taiwan, as our Chinese associates called it. First, our airplane would be a long way inland. Hours later it would be too submerged for continued

Our quarters in Deetah, the police station. Our party took over the left side of the building, and a detachment of Chinese guerrillas took over the right side.
(Photo by Winborn)

The house we commandeered at Pirate's Bay. It had barred windows to keep the pirates out. (Photo by Winborn)

inspection. Perforce, we got in some Pacific Ocean swimming while performing our duty.

While all of this was going on, we had to find quarters and subsistence. The village was right on the coast, which meant that pirates could be a problem. The place was sometimes called Pirates' Bay. All of the houses were of stone construction with heavily-barred windows. We picked out one of the better ones and invited the occupants to live somewhere else for a few days. We didn't much care for their wok, so we took over the wok and charcoal stove in a nearby house.

The first night someone gave us a fish. We cooked rice on our wok. Then we cooked fish. After that we boiled water for the tea. The tea tasted fishy. So we learned that the correct procedure is to first cook the fish, then the rice, and then boil the water for the tea. Rice absorbs the fishy taste and imparts very little flavor of its own. When the tide was out the Chinese dug oysters from the beach. They were a most welcome addition to our standard rice and eggs diet.

My bedroom was on the second floor with only one door, which opened onto a porch—a *cul de sac*. It actually had a bed. I put up my mosquito tent. Sometime during the night we were all awakened by a loud challenge from one of our sentries—*"Nah gah!"* There was no response. A louder *"Nah gah!"* followed, accompanied by the slamming of rounds into the chambers of tommy guns. False alarm—it was only the village drunk coming home too besotted to answer a challenge.

Whenever I awakened during the night I could hear a rat gnawing in the timbers overhead. In the morning my face was covered with very fine wood dust that had sifted through the mosquito netting. It brushed off without any trouble—quite early in the day.

What with pirates around and plenty of Japanese in the vicinity, the site was far from secure. So we were provided with a personal bodyguard of six Chinese guerrilla troops who also had been trained by the US Navy. One day the soldiers shot a heron. I don't know what they did with the feathers, but nothing else went to waste. They meticulously turned the intestine inside out, washed it in well-used water, cut it into short lengths, and tossed the pieces into their wok, along with all of the other chunks of the bird. When it was cooked, they graciously offered

Janasky and "Frank." (Photo by Winborn)

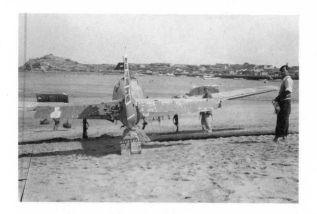

When the tide went out, "Frank" was high and dry, and at first in surprisingly good condition. Willie with "Frank."

Willie with "Frank"

Willie with "Frank" and "helpers." (Photos by Winborn)

Millard and Winborn continue working as tide comes in.
(Photo by Janasky)

Left to Right: Millard, Janasky, Winborn, "Frank." China bowls of rice and
eggis, eaten with chopstocks. (Photo by Willie)

Winborn and Millard starting to dismantle "Frank." (Photo by Janasky)

Soldiers carrying a piece of "Frank" back to the police station at Deetah.
(Photo by Winborn)

Millard and Janasky at Deetah Police Station, along with "Frank's" cowling.
(Photo by Winborn)

Millard with part of
"Frank" at Deetah Police
Station. (Photo by
Winborn)

to share the feast with us. We thanked them but said that we didn't want to deprive them of any of their treat.

We were sorry to leave that lush resort out on the coast. Believe me, we stayed in worse places on the way home.

The pilot of the Frank had survived the perilous period beginning when his airplane first skidded to a stop, but only because some Chinese soldiers happened to be right there. These soldiers had been trained to keep the populace away from prisoners until after they had been interrogated. I was selected to conduct the interrogation, which was held in Putien.

The pilot was large for a Japanese and quite good looking. He still wore his flight suit, simply because the Chinese did not have any clothing large enough to fit him. He said that he was just a ferry pilot who flew new airplanes from Shanghai to Taiwan and that he had become lost. Taiwan was on the other side of the strait on whose shore he had landed. We asked him why, if he were just a ferry pilot, did he carry all that potent twenty millimeter ammunition. His answer did not interpret well. He was convincing on all other matters. It became quite obvious that he knew that his country could not win this war and that he felt he would be happier on the other side. We could empathize with that.

Interpretation was difficult. My interpreter could handle Chinese and quite a lot of English. We found a Chinese soldier who was bilingual in Chinese and Japanese. The stumbling block was that the Chinese language did not include a technical vocabulary. The Japanese had built up a technical glossary based largely on the Japanization of English words. For example, they started with the English word "flap." Japanese people had great difficulty in making the "l" sound. So "flap" became "furap," except that neither the Japanese nor the Chinese liked single-syllable words. So they called a "flap" a "furappu." I had had some training in this sort of thing.

The interrogation covered a lot of territory. I'll mention just one item here. Our colleagues in the Pacific had learned the piston displacement of the Frank's eighteen-cylinder radial engine. We could estimate its rotational speed quite closely by the pitch of the sound it made. The pitch was high—the Japanese were able to operate at a somewhat higher RPM than we were. If only we knew how much boost they were able to use for high power operation (take-off, for instance) we could estimate how much power they could get out of their engines. "Boost" was compression of the intake air by the super-charger. With higher boost, more charge could be packed into the combustion chambers. More power would be generated by the engine, provided of course that it did not disintegrate. We Americans measured boost in units of inches of mercury ("in. Hg.").

I got across the concept of "take-off" very readily by pantomiming, but my tenuous channel of interpretation simply could not cope with "boost" or "manifold air pressure." So I picked up a pencil and drew a neat sketch of the impeller of a supercharger. Before I had time to add the casing, the Japanese broke in and said, "Oh, imperrer." I decided to try by-passing a lot of interpretation by putting down a blank, followed by "mm Hg," using metric units as the Japanese did. The pilot immediately filled in the blank. The number he gave was believable but just barely so. It was higher than our engines would tolerate. I sent the information back to Washington.

If that pilot and I had ever met under more propitious circumstances, we might have become good friends. As it turned out, I was to encounter him once again.

On our way back to Mintsing, our party of five, including two interpreters, walked hard all one day. We were tired and we were hungry. We got into a village late that afternoon. A local merchant had a large glass jar full of deep-fried peanuts on the counter of his little stall. We asked, "Could we sample the peanuts?"

"Of course." The peanuts really hit the spot. He gave us a price on the whole jar. We countered with an offer of about one third that much. We had some more samples. Much negotiation. Eventually the merchant had come down in his price and we had upped our offer until we were within a small fraction of one cent gold of a meeting of the minds. Impasse. More samples. Neither party would make that last concession. Finally, I said to one of our interpreters, "Tell the merchant that if he doesn't meet our offer very soon, he no longer will have any merchandise left to sell." The merchant looked over at his jar. More than three-quarters of the peanuts were now gone. He came to our terms right then and we paid him. No other system of commerce works nearly as well as the free market.

Coming back upstream, our boat was unable to ascend the rapids in the river without help. A large harness, with places for about a hundred trackers, was brought out. One end was attached to the boat, and taking their places in the harness, the coolies strung out along a trail on the river bank. With all of them straining, encouraged by a plaintive song, our great ship was hauled up the rapids.

We anchored for the night at Suikoh. A funeral was underway, with lots of noise to scare away the demons—firecrackers, noisemakers, and interminable playing of tunes on a two-stringed violin. One of the tunes haunted me—I finally recognized it as "The Merry Widow Waltz."

We were gone three weeks on this trip.

7
Miss Wallace

AND

Willie Ho

The Educated Youth Army was recruited from the universities. All the recruits thought that they were going to be officers; instead, they were all buck privates. Morale was abysmal. It was rumored that there were some Communist agitators in the ranks. When we had passed through the city of Putien on our recent trip, we found that the Educated Youth Army had gone on a rampage in the towns; so all the civil authorities, including the police, had evacuated. The Educated Youth had moved on, but the police had yet to return.

When we got back to Nanping, we learned that the Educated Youth Army was now there, having moved in with the local Chinese garrison. A day or so after we returned, Lucas's outfit put on some kind of a production in an auditorium they had. They invited one hundred Educated Youth to be their guests. Two hundred showed up, and the hundred who couldn't get in went on another rampage, causing considerable property damage.

While we were eating dinner the next night, we heard sudden wild screams from the girls' school. We rarely saw any of the girls, but being the closest military, we considered ourselves to be their special protectors. All six of us rushed out. I was still so green that I hadn't bothered to put on my .45. Chico, our houseboy, intercepted me and pantomimed that I must get my gun.

Two hundred Educated Youth were trying to stage a mass rape at the school. A number of them had already climbed the hill and scaled the wall around the compound. Our team opened fire and fairly quickly overpowered those who were already in the compound. One of our chiefs shot an Educated Youth in the buttock with his revolver.

After the gunfire broke out, the mayor pulled a *jing bao*, as was customary, so that he could plunge the town into darkness without losing face. The situation within the courtyard was soon under control, but hordes of soldiers were still swarming up the hill. I was one of our unit taking up a position at the wall and shooting down into the soldiers climbing up. They had good tree cover. Soon word was passed around that none of the Educated Youth were armed, and we holstered our weapons. We could pick bricks out of the top of the wall and bounce them off the heads of the climbing soldiers. The bricks were perhaps more devastating than the weapons. Our only thought was to stop the assault.

It was almost dark when someone blew a call on one of those weird Chinese bugles, and the Educated Youth faded away into the night. The gun-shot soldier put his arms over two comrades' shoulders and they carried him down the hill. When we made a thorough search for any possible stragglers we found the rice straw sandals the wounded soldier had been wearing, pointing toward the school building. He had literally been shot out of his shoes.

With order restored, Miss Wallace called a muster. One girl was missing. Miss Wallace decided to get a flashlight and go down into the town to look for the missing girl. I took another flashlight and accompanied her. I had my .45 drawn, round-in-the-chamber, full cock. If a toad had jumped out, it would have been blasted. The blackout was one hundred percent. Not one soul was on the streets of Nanping, which was unheard of. We searched everywhere we could think of and found nothing. Finally, after about two hours, we reluctantly trudged back up the hill. The next morning brought brighter news. The missing girl had come back unharmed. She had been down in the town when the gunfire broke out and had sought refuge in the home of some friends.[1]

The general in command of the local garrison called Lucas and said, "I trust that in the event of any further disturbance on the part of the Educated Youth Army, this time the Americans will refrain from using firearms."

Lucas called the local general's superior, a higher ranking general up the line, and gave a calm report on the incident. The higher ranking general called the local general and really chewed him out.

The local general called Lucas and said, "I trust that in the event of any further disturbance on the part of the Educated Youth Army, this time the Americans will shoot to kill."

The local general got trucks and hauled the Educated Youth Army a few kilometers out of town. He picked out six of them. "You —you— you—you—and you and you," and had their heads chopped off. We never saw or heard from the Educated Youth Army again.

We were careful not to let any hint of the incident creep into the reports that we sent up through our channels. Curiously, our topside never queried us about it.

Tokyo Rose picked up the story and went on the air bleating about the "Battle of Nanping. Brutal American Officers Fire into Unarmed Chinese Troops." Well, let's see . . . .

About ten days after I had interrogated the Japanese pilot in Putien, I encountered him again, this time right in Nanping. A detachment of Chinese soldiers had brought him up the river. He was still dressed in his Japanese flight suit, and the soldiers had great difficulty in protecting him because the local Chinese kept pegging rocks at him. The soldiers turned him over to an OSS unit stationed near our home base.

I was called in to do the interrogating. This time it was very simple—I had the services of a highly competent interpreter—Staff Sergeant George T. Yamamura, USA, who had joined our TAI unit while I was away on the recent trip. Actually I didn't learn much more about the Frank airplane than I had before, but the pilot gave me a wealth of information about a forthcoming Japanese missile, which I sent on to Washington.

We could not have operated at all without our interpreters. The Chinese Nationalist Government insisted that we let it furnish our interpreters, gratis, as part of its contribution to the war effort. Then the

Government could feel sure that it would know all about everything that we said or did.

No way!

The Government did not furnish clerks, so we hired, at our own expense, clerks—clerks who could interpret. We coined a name for these clerks. We called them "interpreters."

Ho Chin Chia was the name of the interpreter found for me by some veterans in my outfit. He asked to be called "Willie Ho."

He was from Hong Kong—young, slight, attractive. He told me, "I am a good Christian boy." Neither of us, particularly me, witnessed for Christ very well during our travels. We endured many hardships together and sallied forth into regions where security was, at best, problematic. We engaged in countless prolonged negotiations. He found our way flawlessly over long distances of trails and rivers, and never complained or held back from entering into any of my more dubious ventures.

One time we spent a couple of hours trudging up a mountain. On top, the trail forked. Two well-carved stone markers had been set into the ground at the fork. On one of them I could read the character for "right" and the name of a village. On the other, the character for "left" and the name of another village. One of the villages was the one we wanted to go to. So the markers were very helpful, except that the marker for "right" was planted by the left fork and vice versa.

"Well, Willie," I said, "which fork do we take?"

He thought only a few moments and then selected one of the forks. Twenty *li* further on we arrived at the proper village.

That evening, sitting around, I asked, "Willie, how did you know which fork to select up there on the mountain?"

"You mean where those two stone markers were set into the ground?"

"Yes."

"It was simple enough. Whoever had carved those stones was a skilled, educated artisan. His calligraphy was excellent. The coolie who couldn't find anything better to do with his life than lug heavy stones up a mountain, and set them in the ground, obviously was an inferior type."

I couldn't help but reflect that I had just lugged myself up that mountain.

"So of course," Willie continued, "I disregarded what the peasant had done and accepted the input made by the cultured artisan."

Sometimes, when Willie and I were spending the night in an area where security was a bit uncertain, we would put on an act for the surrounding locals that we had rehearsed until we had become impressively adept. Willie would place his loaded carbine across his knees. I would unload my pistol, field strip it, clean and lightly oil every part, then reassemble, replace the clip, pull the slide back, and slam a round into the chamber. Willie would then field strip, clean, oil, and reassemble his carbine, replace the clip, pull the bolt back, and slam a round into the chamber.

Did our little act ever dissuade a dissident from turning us in? I never knew. I do know it was warmly comforting to the two of us.

Willie went everywhere I did until, after the surrender, I finally bugged out of Nanping. When I got back to the States I wrote to him a few times. Then conditions in China deteriorated to the point where I was afraid that it might endanger him to receive personal mail from an American. I stopped writing and lost all contact.[2]

For me, that was very sad.

---

[1] Quite a few months later, when our unit was pulling out of Nanping, Miss Wallace came around and gave each of us a pair of bamboo chopsticks as a token. Except me; she gave me a small box. It contained a lovely little silver spoon, with Chinese designs cut into the handle. I said, "Thank you," and she said, "You're welcome," and we both said, "Goodbye." I am sure we both were thinking of that night months before when we had gone down into the blackedout town looking for a missing girl.

[2] The University of North Texas Press has run an advertisement in two Hong Kong papers in an attempt to locate Willie Ho. As this book goes to press he has not been located. (See Epilogue.)

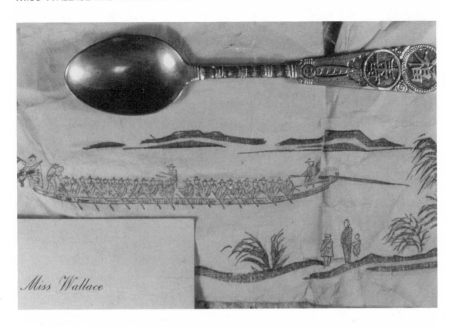

Silver spoon given to Winborn by Miss Wallace. (Photo by Winborn)

8

THE TRIP

TO PINGYANG

Nearly three weeks drifted by with no calls coming in. I hadn't come out to China just to loll around luxurious quarters in Nanping. I decided that the ultimate achievement for a TAI field officer would be to reach a crash site before the pilot did. What a report that would make!

Queries of veterans in Nanping as to where the next plane was most likely to come down pinpointed Linhai, the town I had heard about back in the TAI Center at Anacostia. Linhai was on the coast as far north as it was possible to go without encountering a particularly mean strain of the enemy.

Willie and I embarked on a Jeep tour of the northern part of my territory.

Kienow, the first stop north of Nanping, was a pleasant little town with a still usable air strip, left over from the AVG days. WASC maintained a comfortable hostel there. It also was headquarters for the Chinese Thirteenth Air Force.

This was an unusual air force in that although it had a warehouse full of pieces of Japanese airplanes, it didn't have any flyable aircraft. I spent some time there with a Chinese officer explaining the function of Technical Air Intelligence. I suspect that my lecture had very little effect on the overall war effort.

We touched base with the SACO unit in Kienyang, and then drove to the extreme northern edge of my territory and stopped over at the AGAS outpost in Shangjao. Our hosts were civilized types. They had found something to mix with the raw rice brandy that made it a presentable libation for the cocktail hour. On the staff was a truly beautiful

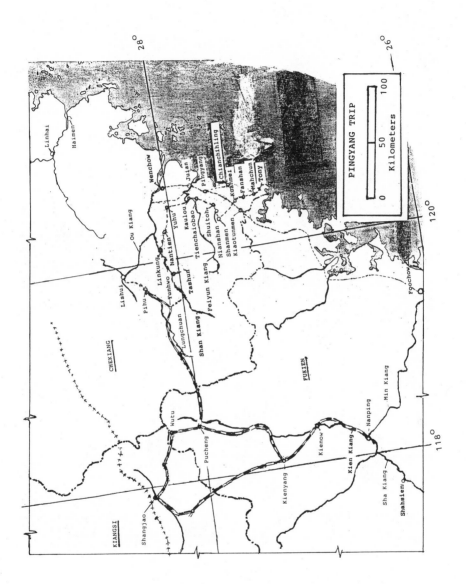

Pingyang Trip. (Map by Winborn)

Ferry across a river north of Kienyang. The steep-sided hill across the river is
typical of those on top of which, according to Chinese folklore, are found tea shrubs
whose leaves produce a particularly choice grade of tea. Due to the difficulty of
harvesting these tea leaves, monkeys (who happen to be white) are trained to
identify this shrub and used to harvest the leaves, bringing them out in little baskets
strapped to their tummies. I am not in a position to say whether or not there is any
validity to this legend, but I have been served Fukien White Monkey tea and
it was delicious. (Photo by Winborn)

Eurasian girl; English father and Chinese mother. Slender, shapely, black hair, light complexion, with enough Oriental charm to add fascination. She brought back memories of girls we had known in far away places. She was fun to talk to; but you mustn't touch. The major who ran the establishment kept her on a very close tether.

War annals are supposed to feature long passages about torrid encounters with glamorous women. The reader may have detected a dearth of such material in this recital.

Well, let's see, there was Miss Wallace. For no one did I have greater admiration. But our relationship was hardly a romance. I suppose that there may have been some superior, attractive girls in Southeast China. If so, they were kept well hidden—with good reason, no doubt. The total number of Red Cross women, USO girls, WACs, nurses, press correspondents, tourists—you name it—in the whole area was precisely zero. Chinese prostitutes, mostly rougher than a cob, were readily available if you cared for that sort of thing, and some of the fellows did in spite of their coarse mannerisms, with very little evidence of any daintiness. It was also possible to buy a few peasant girls and set up a social club, but when you tired of them you could not sell them back to their families. You could not give them back. Oh, no! They were no longer marketable merchandise, but would have to be supported for the rest of their lives. You were required to pay the families to take them back.

Ah, well. Romantic encounters with passionate women were among the many things that were said to occur in other theaters of war.

The headquarters of the Chinese Third War Zone was located at Wutu. Willie and I put up at the AGFRTS outpost there. We had time to spare and a few of us indulged in some target practice with an M1903 Army Springfield rifle. Chinese boys would scramble for the hot shell cases as they were ejected. Brass was precious. My shoulder showed the effects of our practice the following day.

Willie and I spent a night at the British Military Mission in Pucheng. The next morning one of the British officers and I stood on the heights overlooking the parade grounds. Four companies of Chinese troops

Young girls for sale by their step-amah. Their families could not afford to keep them. (Photo purchased from a street vendor in Shanghai.)

were lined up at attention. One soldier was called forward and ordered to stick out his right arm, palm up. A sergeant brought down a heavy club with a blow which broke all of the soldier's fingers over backward. The blow was repeated just to make sure. The same punishment was inflicted on the left hand. Then as the crowning indignity, the sergeant ripped all insignia off the soldier's chest, including the cloth patch with his name, rating, and serial number in indelible ink. The former soldier was   dismissed.

The miserable soul was now hopelessly crippled without useable hands. Anyone who assisted him would have to take care of him for the rest of his life. Chinese custom was absolutely rigid on this matter. No ordinary family could sustain a non-productive member. There was no such thing as a Chinese agency which might assist him. We foreigners had learned in no uncertain terms that we were not to intervene in internal Chinese affairs. The cripple stumbled away in pain to find a place to die.

The British officer and I walked away in silence.

Lieutenant Reno, one of the marines with whom I had spent a night at the Air Force hostel in Algiers, turned out to be an Old China Hand (OCH). In the morning I honed and stropped my Rolls razor with great clackety-clack. The OCH said, "You won't be able to use that razor out where you are going. The Japanese would hear it." When I got out into the area where I thought I might be heard, I stopped shaving and grew a quite impressive Biblical-style beard.

One of the most dismaying aspects of travel on foot would show up when we were unable to find professional carrier coolies in the morning. Under authority vested in us by the Nationalist Government, Willie, with much slapping of the stock of his carbine, would impress "voluntary" civilians to be our coolies for the day. The Government would pay them later.

Rather late one afternoon during the trip, our volunteer coolies were in pathetic shape and we made a prolonged rest stop. We were overtaken by a professional carrier coolie returning home empty. He sized up the situation and took it upon himself to take over the load of our weakest volunteer. He looked at me and said, "I am always glad to help out a Catholic priest."

Catholic priests were probably the most secure individuals there were in that area. I nodded at the coolie and said, "Bless you, my son."

Most of the Chinese found it very difficult to pronounce the sound of the letter "X." Back in Kunming where the fuel for the ground vehicles was a fifty-fifty mixture of gasoline and rice alcohol, we couldn't very tactfully call it "mixed gas." Instead we gave it the much more comfortable name of *"miggis gas."* While traveling, our usual dinner was rice and eggis.

One evening on the trip to Linhai a group of us, part Chinese and part American, were taking turns showing off how much each had learned of the other's language. One Chinese had learned to count in English, "One, du, tree, fo, fi, siggisa"—loud laughter.

He stuck to his guns, "Siggisa: ess-eye-iggisa."

Clearly he had made his point.

Another Old China Hand named Carey ran the AGAS establishment at Yunhwo, the evacuated capital of Chekiang province. When we stopped there, Carey informed me that a Japanese plane was down on the coast in Pingyang District, but that access to it was cut off by the Japanese army retreating northward from Foochow. Furthermore a patrol had been sent out to destroy it. So I decided to continue on my way to Linhai.

We left my Jeep with Carey, got a half-hour ride to Chuchan, and then a ten-hour sampan ride down the Ou Kiang to Lishui. The hotel there was a square, wooden building four stories high. On each floor the toilet was an outrigger affair at a corner—a different corner, of course, for each floor. With this style of architecture it was not advisable to have more than four stories. The outriggers were designed for 110-pound Chinese men, and we massive Americans really clung to something solid when we used one. A large barrel was placed on the ground at each corner, so nothing went to waste, unless the wind was blowing.

Three other Americans from assorted organizations had congregated in Lishui before setting out for Linhai, which was as close to Shanghai as one could get without encountering wall-to-wall Japanese. I still fostered fond hopes of getting to a crash site before the plane's pilot arrived there.

Carey reached me by telephone that evening in Lishui, saying that the plane was now accessible and that the pilot was a prisoner. After spending the night in the hotel, we started back to Yunhwo. The fastest way was via Pihu, which was forty *li* out on a demolished road that could still be walked, although obstructions had been placed across most roads in that area to keep the occupying troops from using them. Vertical earthen mounds fifteen feet high had been placed across the road. Every traveler had to climb a ladder to the top, walk to the far side, and descend another ladder back to the road. In some places deep trenches had been cut across the road. Vehicular traffic was impossible. We were unable to find any carrier coolies, so we hired a coolie with a rickshaw to haul our luggage. It took all of us to get that rickshaw past the obstructions. Carey met us in Pihu and drove us the forty-two kilometers to Yunhwo in my Jeep.

We joined up with Lieutenant Hull, USNR, a member of AGAS, who was going part way in the same direction we were. The trip started with a fifty *li* hike over a big mountain and down to the Shan Kiang. The mountains in this area were larger than I had encountered before. We found a sampan on the river bank, but the boatmen ran off and hid. They came back when Willie yelled, *"mei kuo ren"* (Americans). We drifted downstream for seventy *li*, beaching our craft for the night at Tashun, alongside a bunch of other sampans. The Chinese wouldn't think of mooring a sampan in an isolated stretch of river for the night, any more than they would consider camping out in the beautiful hills rather than sleeping in a bug-ridden hovel in a village. Possibly they were afraid of tigers or bandits, but I think it was mostly because they had always done it that way. The people in the other sampans talked about the Americans all night, and sleep was difficult to come by.

The next morning we cruised seventy *li* to Linkung, a stinking village, where we had to resume foot travel. As soon as we vacated the sampan, its two young boatmen took off up the river. An armed official in another sampan chased and caught them. Maybe our boatmen had neglected to cut the local people in on a squeeze, or maybe it was a draft board action.

The magistrate in the village was preoccupied with processing a document authorizing his soldiers to bring in a dead pig, so he had no time for us. This infuriated Willie, who snatched the pig document from the magistrate's hands and demanded that he get busy finding us coolies. This could be complicated because coolies didn't get paid by Chinese soldiers and in some places they didn't expect to get paid by Americans either. Why not just pay them in advance? Because then they would fade away around the first bend. Willie kept slapping the stock of his carbine until he had rounded up a bunch.

The back stairway of Linkung ran directly up a huge mountain, beyond which the trail went down into a long, sloping valley. The weather was hot and breathless; the air rang with the wails of peasants. Willie said, "They are crying for wind." The breeze sprang up in about an hour.

After a measly fifty *li* walk we reached Nantien, where we were given fine quarters by the magistrate and found good food in a local restaurant. In the morning I wearied of the slow pace set by Lieutenant Hull and the coolies, and forged on ahead. Willie kept up with me for awhile, then he dropped back and I went on alone. As the *li* rolled by, I came off the mountain following a stream which tumbled down five thousand feet through a beautiful valley in a series of waterfalls. I had some difficulty in getting directions to our destination, Yuhu, because the local people spoke an awful dialect.

In Yuhu we put up at SACO Camp 8. Lieutenant Swentzel, the commanding officer, filled us in on the latest intelligence. The following day we walked on to Kaulou, where we spent the night. We contacted Commissioner Chang, who had evacuated there from the big city of Wenchow. He was most courteous, but obviously uncomfortable about our determination to proceed into a wildly troubled area.

We started walking from Kaulou at 0430 hours, headed for Shuitoh, a town to which Magistrate Chang (not related) of Pingyang District had evacuated. Commissioner Chang provided us with a guard of twenty-four well armed men commanded by a captain, because there were bandits in the area. The guard left us at the end of ten *li*.

At 0830 we reached Tienchiaobao, a sizable Communist town. We went into a restaurant and ordered breakfast. Nobody would serve us, which was most disconcerting. We had no idea what was going on. Finally after a long forty-five minutes, two Chinese soldiers came in and said, "We are to escort you to Shuitoh, where the magistrate will put on a big banquet in your honor this evening." So we gave up the idea of having breakfast. No problem—we would just eat a little extra for dinner.

As we got out of town we encountered six more Chinese soldiers, who now told us, "All the time you were in town, a seventy-five man Japanese patrol was lurking nearby. When they learned that armed Americans were around, they hunkered down and waited. Their orders were to forage for rice—not to mix it up with Americans." The proprietor of the restaurant had known this. He was afraid that they would be antagonized if he served food to Americans.

Magistrate Chang of Pingyang District and the author in Shuitoh, holding hands
like two proper Oriental buddies. Neither one would ever have thought of
holding hands with a woman in public. Note that the author packed his .45 front
left because he found that this gave him the fastest draw.
(Photo courtesy of Magistrate Chang)

Letter from Commissioner Chang
of Kaulou to all local farmers:
"Grow potatoes. The Americans
are coming and they want potatoes,
not rice." This was in reference to
plans for a major American
diversionary landing (called Turkey) on the southeast coast of China prior to the
invasion of the Japanese homeland. The operation never materialized, but at the
time of the Japanese surrender Chiang Kai-shek had moved thousands of his
best troops to the Southeast China coast.

We walked into Shuitoh that afternoon. The magistrate's banquet was indeed superb, with jasmine tea. Chinese people ate seated around the table in proper chairs—none of this crouching on the floor stuff. It had turned out to be a pleasant day for both adversaries in the vicinity. One had acquired rice without any trouble. The other had enjoyed an abundance of fine food. Neither had incurred any casualties.

After the banquet, Willie and I packed lightly for a dash down to the site of the crash. We were almost underway when the magistrate announced that he had just received new intelligence which showed that the route again was blocked and that we must immediately evacuate Shuitoh. We moved back to Nianshan.

When a magistrate wanted to climb up in the world the first thing he did was set up a Department of Foreign Affairs. The Secretary of Foreign Affairs was usually some kid out of Shanghai who spoke an English much more difficult to understand than our own interpreter's. Our present magistrate assigned his Secretary of Foreign Affairs to live with us.

After we had retired for the night, the secretary told us that the magistrate now requested us to pack up and return by night all the way to Kaulou. We couldn't help but feel that we were just as safe in Nianshan as we would be traipsing back to Kaulou, so we just went to sleep. The next day we withdrew another five *li* to better quarters in the school of a village called Shanmen, hired a cook and settled down to wait for those miserable sons of the Rising Sun to get out of our way.

The troops everyone was so concerned about were part of an army that had been garrisoned in Foochow for years and were now retreating northward along the coastal highway, which was not super enough to take a Jeep, but could pass a horse. From time to time the magistrate would send scouts down to see whether they had gone yet. The scouts would come back and report, "We hid in the bushes and watched the Japanese walking by."

I said, "I want to go down and look at those Japanese. Maybe I can get some good pictures."

"All right," the magistrate replied, "I'll get you some coolie clothes and you can go with the scouts in the morning."

"What, look at the Japanese?" Lieutenant Hull's interpreter interjected. "Then they can look at you!"

"Oh, that's right," the magistrate said, and he withdrew his offer. Of course, Willie and I could have gone down anyway if we had had a few scouts, but the only way we could get scouts was through the magistrate. So, being prudent types, we stayed in Shanmen. The magistrate had me billeted in a room on the second floor of a school house in Shanmen—very comfortable.

One of the Kuomintang's programs, for which, in my opinion, it never received proper credit, was to work toward the day when everyone in China would speak the National Language, which we called "*Peiping hua*." It had done so by starting with the youngest classes in school and progressing to the new pupils each year after that. The program had been under way three or four years. Willie and I would often hear whole classes reciting their language lessons in unison in their high-pitched, sing-song voices. When we had to spend a night in some village where the merchants spoke only the obscure local dialect, we would look for kids not over nine years old. Willie would tell them that we wanted rice and eggis. They would scurry off in every direction and run back with our dinner. Shanmen was typical of the areas in which the kids were learning *Peiping hua*.

Most of the locals had never seen an Occidental before. The elders would stand beside the trail and bow respectfully when I walked past— always being scrupulously careful to cover the aggressive right hand with the passive left. The people there had never seen automobiles, Jeeps, or trucks; but everyone had seen airplanes flying overhead.

Basketball was big in China. Football? Baseball? Never heard of them. I had not been much of a basketball player and I hadn't even tried to sink a shot for many years. One morning all the schoolboys were out in the yard shooting baskets. The usual thing—a lineup on each side of the basket with the two groups taking turns tossing the ball. Whoever shot last would go to the end of his line. The kids were good.

I got in one of the lines. Time after time I was lucky if I even hit the backboard. Finally, something happened—I threw a long shot which rimmed the basket three times and then dropped through the net. The kids all cheered as though they had just witnessed the greatest athletic feat ever to be performed in the Orient. I bowed and retired from the exercise.

We spent three days in Shanmen waiting for Japanese troops to get off the road so that we could cross it and move out onto the peninsula where the plane was down. Finally, the scouts reported that the last of them had straggled past. The magistrate, my good buddy, assigned a captain and six soldiers to Willie and me as personal bodyguards. I have never encountered finer troops. I heard that they were usually assigned to anti-communist activities. The captain and his men were armed with concealed pistols; Willie carried his carbine, and I packed my automatic. We weren't about to wear uniforms—too conspicuous! The magistrate fitted me out with a conical coolie hat and a weathered rice-straw blouse.

We made the easy walk down to the highway that had been so recently vacated. At the point where we crossed the highway, fifteen *li* north of Kiaotunmen, we found the body of an elderly Chinese gentleman with a wispy white beard. The top of his skull had been bashed in, probably with the butt of a rifle. The blood was barely dry. Most places in Southeastern China were teeming with life, but not this one. The area had a weird aura to it. As my good Christian Willie put it, "Even the demons have left this place."

We walked fifteen *li* farther, approaching Kuanmei. The villagers thought we were returning Japanese and they bugged out. The captain ordered two of his soldiers to overtake them and convince them we were friends. Come on back. Incidentally, we wanted dinner and a place to spend the night. Since we were the first military unit to arrive in Kuanmei after the enemy had moved on, we could, by Chinese custom, have claimed credit for recapturing the town.

We learned that evening what beasts the occupying troops had been—looting, burning the entire town of Kiaotunmen, killing many people and all the livestock they could catch, carrying away and raping young girls. Long ago they had run out of ammunition; but, to keep up appearances, they had filled their ammo boxes with stones and then conscripted civilians to carry them. When a conscript was no longer physically capable of carrying his load, he was disposed of, as we had observed.

The magistrate was very somber for so young a man, because many of his people had been raped and killed during the last few days. The only time his face lit up was when someone mentioned that, while the Japanese were there, their general had learned that both his wives and all his children had been killed in a B-29 raid on Tokyo.

We had crossed the road, but the enemy were still uncomfortably close. That night Willie and I went through our gun-cleaning routine to dissuade any possible dissidents from getting ideas.

The peninsula we were walking into the next day was strictly outlaw country. My friend, the magistrate of Pingyang District, had wisely refrained from sending his soldiers into the area. As we trod onward through the steady rain, Willie told me about the town, Fanshan, that we were approaching. It once had been a prosperous mining town by a mountain which was, of all things, composed of alum. "Fanshan" means "Alum Mountain." But for the past several years the mining business hadn't been good, and by now nearly everyone in the area had become an outlaw of one breed or another—robber, bandit or pirate. They all stole, but robbers operated alone or in pairs. Bandits were members of a well organized, more or less respected clan, and pirates operated at sea.

After several hours walk we crested a hill and looked out over the large valley in which Fanshan was situated. A mob of troops in white uniforms was milling around a temple. What in the world were we getting into this time? The guards shoved me into a rest shelter beside the trail because I was conspicuous by being so outlandishly tall. The captain sent two soldiers out to reconnoiter. They came back and reported that the troops were what Willie called "Big Knife Bandits." I have read books referring to them as "Broad Sword Bandits."

I began to learn about Big Knife Bandits, who were very clannish. They wore their own uniform, mostly white, and a hat with a dash of red on it. They had their own flag, a red affair with a complicated device of silver stars. Big Knife Bandits were not Communists; it was simply that red was their favorite color. They had their own religion, and, at intervals, would face the sun and bow with palms pressed together in front of their chests. They robbed only the rich and the magistrates and so were quite well regarded by the common people. Until very recently these bandits had been Japanese puppets. But the Chinese Nationalist Government had scored a great coup by winning their allegiance. This triumph involved a grant of amnesty for past sins and a cash payment—probably amounting to a few cents gold—to each bandit. Besides, the bandits could see the handwriting on the wall. The Nationalists were going to win.

Since the bandits were now our allies, it was quite permissible to fraternize with them. We formed our party of nine armed officers and men into a column and came marching resolutely down the mountain. Would the bandits treat us as allies or as the fortuitous victims of their next robbery of the rich? Neither—they formed into a column of fours and marched in good order out the other end of the valley with flags flying.

We entered the town, which was as crooked and cramped a place as I have ever visited. The narrow streets were hemmed in by heavily walled buildings with small barred windows. We called on the magistrate, who invited us to be his guests for the midday meal, a thought we had in mind ourselves. We had spent some forty-five minutes with this magistrate when a courier rushed in breathlessly with a written message which informed the harried official that a party of nine enemy soldiers, one with a rifle and eight with pistols, was approaching his town. We allayed his fears by explaining that we were the nine "Japanese," the rifle being the carbine that I had Willie carry.

After we had eaten, the magistrate mentioned casually, "The Japanese airplane that you are after came down quite near the coast. Pirates wanted to get the guns. So they have been brought to my town and hidden here."

"Good," I said. "Guide us out to where they are so I can make rubbings of the markings on their receivers and collect one sequence of ammunition."

"No."

"You will remember that I showed you my pass chopped by General Chennault, authorizing me to make such inspections."

"I cannot have your party guided out to those guns."

"Why not?"

"Because the Big Knife Bandits are trying to get the guns. If your party is taken out to them, the Bandits will learn where they are hidden and will capture them when you have moved on."

"I was under the impression that we just chased the Bandits out of your valley."

"They still have agents here who will report to them everything that goes on."

It was raining like mad. We negotiated for two hours before finally making a deal. I convinced him that one coolie with one small boy walking in the rain would not attract the Bandits' attention. He got a small boy to guide me out to the guns, and I wore my coolie clothes. The guns (12.7 millimeter machine guns) were hidden in the temple that the Bandits had been milling around when we first saw them.

That afternoon the trail led up into mountains with many curves. As was usually the case, you would walk at your own preferred speed. You would often pass completely out of sight of your friends. Suddenly, you would round a curve and find yourself face-to-face with a Big Knife Bandit armed with an iron-tipped spear. Had anyone told him that we were allies? Did he know how to use that spear? You and the bandit would each stare straight ahead, pass, walk exactly four more paces, and then irresistibly wheel around to see if the other guy was going to start something. Deciding that the answer was negative, each of you would resume course in his original direction. Some of the Bandits were armed with the traditional big knives. Not all of our allies in World War II had state-of-the-art weaponry.

That evening we reached Mahchun, the town nearest the crash, and called on Magistrate Wong, who very kindly gave me the bed in his office. He moved into his wife's quarters for the first time in years. He had a group photograph taken of himself, his son, the captain, Willie and me. He served some excellent Japanese beer recovered from a ship that the Americans had sunk out in the bay. I hadn't had any beer since leaving the States, and it surely tasted good.

The magistrate had a large desk in his office with a thick plate glass cover under which were dozens of photographs of dead Japanese

A group photograph taken at Mahchun. From the left: Willie, Magistrate Wong with his son, Winborn, and the captain of his guard.
(Photo courtesy of Magistrate Wong)

pilots, including the pilot of the airplane I was after. Mostly they were propped up against trees.

He said that the pirates had tried to steal the plane, and that his soldiers had shot one of them. A number of pieces of the plane had been brought into his quarters and I spent a whole day examining them.

The magistrate explained, "The airplane circled the area with its engine sputtering and then crashed on the brink of a hill overlooking the valley. The pilot lived just fifteen hours, semi-conscious, and in great pain, so no interrogation was possible."

On both of the next two days we walked the fifteen *li* out to the site of the crash. The airplane had been a brand new Tony on a ferry flight. The quality of its manufacture was excellent and it had unusually fair lines.

It appeared to me that the crash should have been survivable. The airplane had been completely out of fuel so there was no fire. When the pilot's picture was taken, he was still in his flight suit—apparently he had not received much medical attention during those reputed last fifteen hours.

While I was under instruction at MIT, my powerplants professor expounded on the great superiority of fuel-injection systems over the carburetor systems used in American airplane engines. Being something of a novice, I asked, "Why, then, don't the Americans use the fuel-injection systems?" The professor's reply was a slightly sanitized version of, "Why, you stupid jerk, only the Germans have the superb machine tools and the master machinists required to handle the precision tolerances of a fuel-injection system."

The Tony bore a marked similarity to the superb German Messerschmitt Bf. 109. Its engine was an inverted twelve cylinder Vee, built under license to Daimler Benz. One report indicated that the Germans had furnished their Axis partner with a complete set of drawings and specifications for the airplane, delivered to Tokyo Bay by submarine. The engine was a good copy—except that the Japanese had thrown out the German design for the fuel injection pump and developed an improved version of their own.

I did some engine work and dismounted the fuel injection pump, which had fourteen tubes sticking out, and lashed it to a bamboo pole so that it could be toted away by a couple of coolies.

This task left my hands all grimy, costing me a definite loss of face. Certainly all superior persons had servants to perform such menial tasks.

It was a wonderful relief after a hard day's walk on cobblestones to remove the boots, soak the feet, and then put on clean socks and light sandals for the rest of the day. The rubber from a Japanese self-sealing tank made the best sandal soles in the world, unbelievably tough, durable and resilient. A Chinese shoemaker back in Nanping could attach neat pigskin uppers.

In American airplanes, the rubber of the self-sealing fuel cells was placed inside the aluminum tanks. When a bullet penetrated a tank, the aluminum tended to "petal" and hold the wound open. The Japanese placed the rubber on the outside of the aluminum tanks—no petalling problem. They used beautiful natural rubber from the Malay Peninsula or maybe from the Netherlands East Indies, not some synthetic material concocted out of butadiene curds. Why didn't the bullet petal their tank at the exit wound? Liquid gasoline is very effective at tumbling a bullet and depleting its striking power in a short distance. But what if the tank is empty? Leakage is not much of a problem in an empty tank.

I searched everywhere in the wreckage of the Tony, finding plenty of nameplates, but not a single date. A place for dates was stencilled on the rubber covering of the self-sealing fuel cell, but it had been left blank.

Just before we left a wreck, it was customary to hack a generous piece of rubber off the fuel tank—enough to take care of sandals for our friends as well as for us.[1] The stuff was so tough to cut with a knife that invariably the hacker's fingers would be dripping blood from many small cuts before he finished. I made the sacrifice. Under the ample piece of rubber removed was a date stencil on the metal tank with the date filled in. This calibrated the whole airplane.

The weather was getting hot and I didn't relish the idea of a long walk up the coast to the Ou Kiang, which flowed down from Lishui. So

I spoke to the magistrate, saying, "Please get me a junk so that I can sail up the coast in comfort."

"No."

"I'll pay."

"No."

"Why not?"

"There are pirates in the bay."

"I don't give a damn about pirates. I have a crack nine-man armed party."

"The pirates have a seventy-five millimeter cannon on their junk."

"We'll set out walking the first thing in the morning."

We had a little time to spare, so I said, "Willie, let's get in some target practice." Sometimes this was a good idea in a spot where the security was somewhat iffy. We were both good shots. The magistrate was duly impressed. He had apprehended a couple of low-down robbers and wanted them taken up to Pingyang to get their heads chopped off. We obviously were the most potent military force in his sector and since we were going to Pingyang anyway, he turned the two robbers over to the captain of my guard and got a receipt for them. The felons were evil looking young punks, rather tall for Chinese, with unhealthy complexions. They had been caught killing and had been sentenced.

The next day we walked north. The prisoners were treated well but they were in rotten physical condition and suffered excruciatingly trying to keep up with our ten *li* per hour pace. But if they were going to travel with us, it was up to them to walk as fast as we did. When we stopped at a magistrate's place for a noonday meal, the culprits were left out on the porch with their left wrists tied to a doorknob while we went inside to eat.

I took it upon myself to say, "Willie, aren't those robbers going to escape?"

Willie said, "No."

"But surely they can untie those knots, and anyway that line is very easy to break."

"They won't escape."

"Why not?"

"It isn't done."

Even felons had to abide by Chinese custom.

A Japanese ship had been sunk by the Americans in shallow water nearby, and the Chinese had recovered many bottles of Formosan fruit juice, which added the perfect touch to a truly delightful meal.

That afternoon we moved into territory taken over completely by the Big Knife Bandits. They would cluster around us like a swarm of bees during our rest stops. I could tell that my captain was having a field day regaling them with some kind of story. I found out later that he would point to Willie's carbine and say that it was a super-powerful machine gun. It could fire six hundred rounds "Br-t-t-t!" just like that. The bandit leader was mightily impressed. Then my captain would say, "See that weapon the American carries at his waist?" "A-a-h-h." "One volley can kill one hundred men!" Sucked in breaths. "The flame alone can kill twenty men." Louder sucked in breaths. "See that armament lashed to the bamboo pole?" The bandits would crowd in closer. "Stand back—it is a poison cannon!" They would trip all over themselves backing out of there.

As the sun set, we came off the last mountain onto the edge of a vast level plain, criss-crossed with a network of narrow canals. There were no roads. We knew that Pingyang was only a few hours walk on the other side of the plain, and that my beloved home town of Nanping was, with luck, only seven days hard travel beyond Pingyang.

The Big Knife Bandits had captured Chianchihling at the edge of the plain. They apparently had encountered some slight opposition and had been obliged to burn a few houses. A Chinese Protestant church in the village had been closed. After all, the Big Knife Bandits had their own religion and could hardly be expected to tolerate the presence of some off-beat sect in their own territory. As one of them put it, "Christianity—isn't that a cult that drinks blood?"

A chieftain of the bandits had set himself up as magistrate. He was young, well educated, and reasonably well versed in Chinese etiquette. He was making a good thing out of the bandit business. As was proper, he invited us to dinner. It was always the custom after a dinner for the host to arise and say, "I must apologize for the poor quality of the food tonight," even though it might have been a sumptuous banquet. Then I would rise and make some flowery comment about how delectable the food had been. This host had not as yet whipped his territory into good running order, and the food was just plain awful. So when he arose and presented the customary apology, I responded by saying, "That was truly the finest food I have been served since the last time I ate." I relied on Willie to translate that sentiment into polite Chinese.

By this time the captain and I had become really good friends. He said to me, "Let's not stay in this town overnight. We can hire a few little canal sampans, get ourselves poled across the plain, and walk on into Pingyang in the morning."

"That suits me fine."

We certainly didn't want to take those two scroungy robbers into small sampans with us, so my captain turned them over to the chieftain of the Bandits and got a receipt. It was starting to get dark. I, of course, had nothing to do with the robbers, but I did have an educated opinion as to what their life expectancy at that juncture might be—about fifteen minutes. I didn't hear any gunfire, so I gathered that they had been processed in the traditional manner—heads chopped off. This saved ammunition.

Magistrate Chang of Pingyang District was a warm buddy of mine. He was an excellent host who set a superb table. He enjoyed conversation. A militant type he was not.

The retreating enemy army had straggled on through his home town a couple of days before Willie and I walked in. The magistrate had moved back into his home. He had silverware set out at our places at the table. I had acclimated myself to chopsticks long ago and now found it much more difficult to revert to forks.

The magistrate regaled us with stories of the Japanese behavior during their sojourn in his town. The officers, of course, took over the best houses in town and stabled their horses in the living rooms. In one house, the owner was trapped on the second floor. He managed to hide under the bed. Three officers stretched out on the bed for the night. When the owner heard all three of them snoring, he slipped out and escaped.

This gave me an opening for bugging my friend that I could hardly overlook. I asked the magistrate, "Didn't the owner have a knife? Couldn't he have slit the Japanese' throats while they slept?"

"*Aiee yah!* What a barbaric thought. I get the creeps just thinking about it." The reaction was all that I expected it to be.

Willie and I, walking north on the Coast Road, reached Juian about noon. The last of the army had passed through the day before, and very few of the inhabitants had returned to the town. Willie left me standing on the deserted main street while he scurried around trying to find someone to feed us.

A jaunty, well-dressed, young Chinese showed up and said breezily in good English, "Good afternoon, friend. Have a pack of Polo cigarettes, courtesy of the Philippine-American Tobacco Company. The package looks like Chesterfields."

The next town to the north was the major city of Wenchow, which was on the south bank of the Ou Kiang. The Japanese army, which had been retreating up the road ahead of us, halted in Wenchow and moved in with the garrison already there, so now there were two armies holed up in the town.[2] We would have to make a detour.

My plan was to move far enough inland (west) to avoid this concentration, and then go north until we hit the river, find a sampan there and get on our way toward Lishui. Skirting around enemy armies was not the most pleasant way to live, but I figured that we could keep our eyes open and move briskly. Then if some dissident did report us, we would be gone before a patrol could get there. And if we stumbled across a detachment, well, we could walk faster than they could.

A sluggish river ran inland from Juian. Willie hired us a rather clumsy-looking boat with one boatman and a small boy assistant. The boatman said that we would shove off at 2300 hours, when the tide would start flowing upstream. Two Chinese families with lots of kids and bundles clambered aboard to take advantage of the free boat ride. I had to get some sleep, so I kicked them off.

We set out on schedule. I promptly fell asleep, waking up at 0430. I asked Willie, "Where are we?"

Willie said, "When the tide ceased to flow, the boatman pulled into the bank and stopped. We haven't come very far."

I was furious. Our detour had gotten off to a bad start, and we would be in the area longer than I cared to be. The boatman had his boy get out into three feet of water and try to pull the boat. It was no way to travel. The boatman told Willie, "You can get coolies at a place ten *li* away." Willie walked the ten *li* there and back again on a fruitless trip.

I paid the boy, but refused to give anything to the boatman. Willie finally got coolies and we set out walking. The boatman clung to us for three hours wailing all the way.

We walked all day and that night put up at the home of a farmer who was a sub-magistrate. I had Willie call in our coolies. I paid them and then asked, "Do you know how to get to a landing on the Ou Kiang upstream from where the Japanese are in Wenchow?"

"Yes, yes, yes."

I wanted very much to get to the landing by noon so that Willie could hire a sampan in time for us to be well upriver by nightfall. So I said to the coolies, "I'll give each of you $100 CN extra if you get us to the river by noon tomorrow." They liked the idea of a bonus.

I then asked, "Do any of you have access to a clock?"

"Yes."

"Can any of you read time?"

"Yes."

"Then report here by 0430."

"Good, good, good."

As the coolies went away, their spokesman asked, "Is that before or after the sun rises?"

I fell soundly asleep. In what seemed like a very short time, Willie woke me and said that my coolies were here, ready to start out. It was 0130. Well, let's see now. I had promised them a bonus if they got us to the river by noon, but I hadn't said that they couldn't start a little early. We set out into the night. As it turned out, it was almost noon when we reached the river.

I gladly paid the bonuses.

Willie got us a splendid sampan, with a crew of three boatmen plus a woman to do the cooking and the laundry. She kept that sampan scrupulously clean, and was surprisingly modest. When it was time for her to squat over the gunwale, she would go way forward and rig up a square panel of woven split bamboo to assure her privacy.

At night there was room for all of us to stretch out and sleep. You might say that the sampan operated on the American plan—meals were included. By the second night we reached our destination, Lushui, which means "beautiful water."

Yes, we had selected a roundabout route, but one which took advantage of a lot of water travel.

If you want a peaceful, placid interlude some day, I suggest that you walk to the river's edge and cruise upon the beautiful waters of the Ou Kiang, preferably at a time when the area isn't crawling with enemy troops.

I had sent a telegram to Carey, asking him to have my Jeep in Pihu by noon on the twenty-first, three weeks after I had left it with him to go down the trails to the coast and work over the Tony.

Carey brought Molly Wong with him. They got to Pihu early and had a meal in a local restaurant. Two big baskets were in front of the restaurant, one full of rice, the other full of beans. After Carey and Miss Wong had eaten, a cat jumped up on top of the beans, dug a little hole, answered a call of nature, patted beans over its deposit, and jumped down to the floor. Carey and Miss Wong were disturbed. Carey, an Old China Hand, called the waiter over. *"Gung yo!* That cat just—ah—went in the beans."

The waiter, dead pan, said, "Uh, huh. The cat goes in the beans."

"Well, look," Carey said, "we just had rice with our dinner. Does the cat go in the rice?"

The waiter, with a touch of acerbity, replied, "No, the cat goes in the beans."

Carey insisted on doing the driving on our way back to Yunhwo. Then Willie and I took over my Jeep and set out for Nanping, arriving there five weeks after we had left.

While Willie and I were away on the Pingyang trip, Donald Bellew, Photographers Mate, First Class, USNR, had joined our TAI unit.

Walking past a view the rest of us had walked past many times, he had the knack of spotting something we hadn't noticed, framing the scene with his hands, and coming up with an outstanding photograph.

I also found that Ensign John R. Peppler, USNR, had joined us. We had gone through the school at Anacostia together, and hopped the Atlantic on the same flight. Some way or other he beat me to Cairo. We flew to Karachi on the same transport. I beat him to Calcutta where he spent several months at TAI Center, India. When he finally got to Nanping, Peppler and I roomed together.

---

[1] Twenty-five years later my sandal soles were as good as ever, but the pigskin tops had disintegrated and I had to throw the sandals away.

[2] It must be explained that the term "army" was used very loosely in China. Just about any sizable land-based military unit under one commander might be called an army.

9

EVERYDAY LIFE

IN SOUTHEAST CHINA

An Occidental in China had a pronounced tendency to judge an Oriental by how well that person lived up to Occidental standards. Now maybe American standards are superior to Chinese standards, and maybe not. Great theologians and philosophers could no doubt mull over this matter ad infinitum. But we ordinary people could readily arrive at the conclusion that the standards, philosophies, and religious tenets of the two cultures were indeed profoundly different. For one thing, it appeared that nearly all Chinese believed in reincarnation of the soul— "They can kill me, so what? The next incarnation can't possibly be as bad as this one." And of course demons lurked everywhere. It was not too far-fetched to go on from there and think about how well each culture lived up to its own standards. The disconcerting conclusion would be that, by and large, the Chinese lived up to their standards better than we Westerners did to ours.

On trips to and from the coast we would stop over in Lutu with Mr. Lacy, a Methodist missionary who had spent many years as an evangelist in China. During a long conversation one evening, I asked him, "How does it feel to devote one's life to teaching Christian love to the Chinese and then have Christian Germany and Christian Italy engage in a brutal war with Christian Great Britain and Christian United States?"

He answered sadly, "If you will think for but a few moments, you can answer your question as well as I can."

An ancient burying ground was located on the road from Nanping to Kienyang. Impressive carved stone figures were placed at intervals. Their purpose was to keep the demons away. They were not effective at safeguarding the area from the American barbarians. Winborn is the one on the left.
(Photo by Peppler)

Daring bareback rider. (Photo by Peppler)

Peppler tames one of the beasts. (Photo by Winborn)

Millard selected a slow, comfortable ride. (Photo by Winborn)

Sometimes in Nanping the conversation of an evening would turn to the matter of the best procedure for going out to the latrine on a dark night.

First Profound Thought: "I would hold my flashlight at arm's length. Then if someone shot at me, at least I wouldn't be hit in a vital spot."

Second Profound Thought: "One thing you can be sure of, a Chinese soldier is not going to hit what he is aiming at. I would hold my flashlight right in front of my chest."

Third Profound Thought: "How do you know it will be a Chinese soldier? There are Japanese around here too and they are good shots."

Fourth Profound Thought: "OK, I get the word. I'd stumble out in the dark without any flashlight."

Fifth Profound Thought: "There have been reports of cobras in this area. I'm not about to stumble around in the dark where I might step on a cobra."

I gave an account of this learned discourse to Dr. Warren Anderson, who had been a medical officer in the army during World War II. He asked, "And what was the group's consensus as to the best procedure?"

"Wait until morning."

"I know," he replied. "When I was in the army I treated dozens of constipation cases that started just like that."

Out in the intense heat of Southeast China, our shots—typhoid fever, dengue fever, typhus, bubonic plague, cholera, yellow fever and tetanus, plus a vaccination for smallpox—were thought to play out in six months instead of the usual year. When we would go to Changting for our shots we would see an excellent pharmacist, Sergeant Kittle, and converse with him like we would have with an old family doctor.[1]

Medical officers at stations in the States sometimes had difficulty coaxing all the personnel into taking their shots. This was never the case with the volunteers bound for or already in China. These characters would eagerly take every shot available and clamor for more.

Terribly infectious diseases like yaws erupted in great ulcerated sores. It was said that you could get yaws just by standing downwind of any one of the many victims. Infections caused the eyes to rot and run down the cheeks. At the Chinese opera, likely to be excellent, an usher on a hot night might go up and down the aisle with a basin of hot water. He would wring out wash cloths to be passed from patron to patron for wiping off their sweaty faces. Very refreshing, except that always you would notice that the person who got the cloth just before you did had the eye disease.

The instructions that we were given included:

Don't go swimming—river water carries flukes which spend part of their life cycles in the bodies of snails. These parasites can penetrate your skin and congregate in your liver. The result is shistosomiasis.

Always make sure that your drinking water has been boiled.

Never eat uncooked vegetables or unpeeled fruits. Watermelon may taste delicious on a hot day, but forget the idea of eating any—it is sold by the catty so the farmer may have injected rice paddy water into the melon.

In a restaurant, always have the waiter bring a basin of boiling water so that you can scald your dishes and chopsticks at the table before you use them. Watch out for mosquitoes. Wear long sleeved shirts in the evening no matter how hot it is.

So, it's time to take a bath. Are you sure that you feel dirtier than the wooden basin that is brought for you to bathe in?

Yes, we certainly were concerned over what some of those virulent bugs lurking out there might do to us. But in retrospect, we all did a commendable job of maintaining our precautions against them. One thing that helped was the new army doctor who was popular with the fellows from the moment he arrived.

He was young, athletic, good-looking and extroverted. When trade grew slack in his own town he would hop in a Jeep and sally forth for a week's trip over the great Southeast China Motor Road to care for the ailments of all comers. Usually this meant treating the "GIs," which plagued most of us no matter how often we told our Chinese cookboys not to let the flies and rats tromp all over the pies while they cooled. Doc's treatment was truly heroic. He prescribed and furnished sulfa-guanidine tablets large enough to play checkers with. A good patient in a bad way might require as many as forty tablets in a twenty-four hour session. The physical effort of swallowing forty sulfa-guanidine was nothing to belittle. Vast quantities of *leng kai shui* were consumed in washing them down, and inevitably Chico, our houseboy, would have to stoke up the fire and boil extra batches of water all day. The theory of the treatment seemed to be that if enough concrete were dumped into the patient, it would plug up the leak in his plumbing. Personally, I did not go along with Doc on this sulfa-guanidine treatment, but much preferred a Chinese potion that was loaded with chloroform and opium and was most delectable to take.

"Chico," Wong and Chen, our servants in Nanping. Some American had given "Chico" the name and it stuck. Chico was the houseboy and was full-grown. Wong was a good cook, and Chen was a coolie who toted the groceries, etc.
(Photo by Bellew)

Doc took one of his trips up north. Returning from it, he jockeyed his Jeep into Nanping one afternoon. He looked as though he had been dragged behind the vehicle for the last hundred kilometers. What little clothing he wore was tattered and greasy. His person was covered with the dust of three provinces. It was presumed that he was deeply sun-tanned under it all. He had been having the normal run of trouble with his Jeep, and in Southeast China everyone was his own Jeep mechanic. During this trip the rear universal joint on the front drive shaft had let go, allowing the liberated end of the shaft to thrash around under the vehicle with colossal sound effects until it jammed, which of course locked the front wheels and ground the little truck to a halt in a cloud of dust. Doc's diagnosis indicated that the only hope of saving his mount was to amputate the drive shaft. He performed the operation on the spot, and resumed his journey on the rear drive shaft. A little later, the horn went out on him. Driving a silent Jeep in China resulted in more casualties than really could be tolerated, so Doc had been forced to remove the muffler. It is surprising that he had a muffler, because, like shock absorbers, they were one of those refinements that were said to be used in other theaters of war.

We refused to have any part of mufflers on our own Jeeps. Our technique for negotiating Chinese villages was to gun the rig up to a thundering thirty-five, slam her into second and let off on the gas. We would then careen down the cramped street with a salvo of violent backfires that shooed the chickens, children, coolies, and pigs in all directions. One of the riders would then look back and tally up the score— two chickens confirmed, one pig probable. Near misses didn't count. I suppose Doc had wanted to use the horn instead of the backfire all the time. On top of the drive shaft and muffler jobs, Doc had been obliged to take care of five flat tires during his run.

He came up to our place that afternoon, and we sat around waiting for the ice cream to harden. Yes, ice cream! Nanping was widely famous as the town where ice was available. The Americans trooped in from hundreds of kilometers around to gorge upon fine Nanping "buffalo milk" ice cream.

Our conversation with Doc while we waited, revealed the startling fact that he had been born in China. As he put it, "My parents took me to the States at the age of one. I stayed there for twenty-five years. Now that I'm twenty-six, the army has sent me back to China. And you know," he added, "those were the happiest twenty-five years of my life."

The rich life of the street, in Changchow in this instance. Chicken, duck, kid scratching himself, coolie with yoyo pole, tray for blowing the chaff off rice, and lots of people. Just blow a series of backfires and plough on through.
(Photo by Mattmiller)

At an elaborate dinner on one of my trips, my host plunged his chopsticks into the big chicken dish and fished out a head to put on my plate. Eyes were particularly choice, and one could crush the skull with his teeth and suck out the brains. For seconds, I was served the prized feet. Some Chinese colonel who had been brought in just to fill up the table was relegated to eating the insipid white meat.

An American friend and I had an hour or so to spare sitting in the yard at his intelligence outpost. A cookboy came around and proudly showed us a young rat that he had caught. The rodent was nailed to a small piece of board. The cookboy was trying to pet the animal because it was soft and sleek. The rat was trying to bite the cookboy's finger because it didn't like that nail through its right hind foot. My host asked if that were dinner for tonight. The cookboy gave an enthusiastic yes. This establishment had separate messes for the Americans and the Chinese. The meat dish for the Americans that night was tough water buffalo. I favored the larger hunks.

Restaurants typical of those we used when on a trip. The meat served during a day was slaughtered early in the morning. This was a slow and apparently very painful process. Hunks of fresh meat were hung from the ceiling of the place until they were chopped up and thrown into the wok. There was, of course, no refrigeration. (Photos by Mattmiller)

We stopped for a noonday meal one day with a minor magistrate who had not expected us. It was a swampy region. He sent some kids out to scrounge for food. The result was a frog and turtle dish. The turtle meat was cut into pieces, but the small frogs were thrown in whole. They now floated around in the soup with their little eyes bugging through the surface. One frog made a nice sized mouthful. I ate mostly turtle.

An AGFRTS friend said that he had been a guest recently at a dinner having a main course of eels six or seven inches long. While still alive, the eels were put into a wok full of cool water. The wok was placed on a charcoal stove and covered with the wooden lid. As the water heated up the eels would get uncomfortable and bump their heads against the lid. When they stopped bumping, they were done. Several eels were served on my friend's plate. One was a little rare and recovered, slithering off his plate and out across the table. He said that he never had much liked eel and that now he didn't care for it at all.

But in all fairness, I am only too glad to report that, in my opinion, the best Chinese cooking is the best cooking in the world. Take for example shark fin soup, which was served at most fine banquets. The fins of a shark have a stringy structure resembling lengths of a gelatinous spaghetti laid together side-by-side. This foodstuff could be dried so that it would keep indefinitely. Forty-eight hours of soaking, simmering, and fussing were required to convert the dried material into a soup that was beyond comparison.

The rule was, whatever you were served, if it tasted good, you enjoyed it and never asked what it might be, even if it might be Cantonese cat and snake soup.

It was reported that in most theaters of war the GI's scorned the Spam that was included so generously in their rations. Our airlift was too meager to furnish such items to those of us in Southeast China, but somehow or other I occasionally got hold of a can. Some Spam tossed into my evening's rice would glorify the whole day.

One of the many stories heard around Nanping was about the five sourdoughs wintering over in a crude shelter in Alaska. They all hated to do the cooking. The cardinal rule of the place was that if anyone criticized the grub, he would immediately become the next cook. One night Edgar started eating and remarked, "This soup tastes like urine—but good, but good!" "But good" became a familiar part of our lingo. Many aspects of life in China were proclaimed to be "but good."

At most inns and magistrates' places a bed was a few planks laid across two sawhorses. I was most fortunate in that shortly before I left the States a friend gave me his Boy Scout sleeping bag with an air mattress. A khaki army GI wool sweater served as my pillow, under which I always put my .45.

AGAS and the Office of War Information collaborated in publishing a "Pointie Talkie" booklet printed in China. The basic format was to show in the first column a question or a request in English, in the second column the same item in Chinese, in the third column one or more answers in Chinese, and in the fourth column the same answers in English. Thus an American could point to an item in the first column and his Chinese collaborator could point to the appropriate answer in the fourth column.

One item in the first column was, "Please ask these people staring at me to go away." The passage continued, "Don't expect this to work like magic."

It didn't. Quite often a crowd of local Chinese would stand around awestruck over all of the preparations the American made going to bed. I would start blowing up my air mattress by mouth and one of the locals, wanting to be helpful, would take over and blow it up about as hard as the planks it rested on. I had to use it that way—I could hardly cause him to lose face by partially deflating it right after he had worked so hard blowing it up.

One of the last steps was to make sure that the mosquito tent was tucked in all around and then go over every square inch of its inner surface with a flashlight and kill any mosquitoes that might have hidden inside.

I have skipped the most important part, which was to dust the interior of the sleeping bag with some of the contents of a little olive-drab can issued by the United States Army and labeled: "Powder, Insecticide, for Body-Crawling Insects." Occasionally, if I didn't go to

B.R. WINBORN, LT. USNR

POINTIE
TALKIE

中美協力爭取勝利

Pages from Winborn's "Pointie Talkie" booklet printed in China.

CHINESE SECTION

Before using, show the Chinese to whom you
want to get an idea across the Chinese text at
the top of the opposite page. Then for your question, point to the Chinese writing on the same
line as the English language idea you want to
put across. In reply, the Chinese will point to
the phrase he wishes to use as an answer. All
questions are on left-hand pages; answers on
right-hand pages.

I. FINDING AN INTERPRETER

1. Is there someone here who can speak   這裏有人會說

    English?   英文嗎？
    French?   法文嗎？

2. Is there any foreigner in the vicinity who is willing to co-operate with you in helping me?   這附近有肯與我們合作的外國人來幫忙我嗎？

3. Will he come here?   他能到這裏來嗎？

CHINESE SECTION

親愛的中國朋友們：

我是美國軍官，來到中國幫助抗戰，但是我不會說中國話，倘若我問你甚麼話，我指着這本書上左邊的問話，請你指着右邊的答語，很正確的答覆我。

有。   1. Yes
沒有。   No.
我不知道。   I don't know.

有。   2. Yes
沒有。   No.
我不知道。   I don't know.

他能來。   3. Yes.
他不能來。   No.
我不知道。   I don't know.

11. Please ask these people staring at me to go away; I want privacy. (Don't expect this to work like magic.)

請你告訴這些人不要圍着看我。

....

12. I would like to borrow these.
I shall send them to you later on.

我想借這些東西用用。

我用完了就立刻奉還。

....

13. Please bring me another blanket.
More clothes.

請給我多拿一張毯子或棉被來。

多拿點衣服來。

....

14. I'd like to keep my shirt on.
Trousers.
Shoes.
And put Chinese clothing over them.

我想我還穿上我自已的衣服。

褲子。

鞋子。

但是外面再加上點中國衣服。

....

可以的。

對不住，我們也要用這些東西，所以不能出借。

12. Alright.

Sorry, we have to use them too, therefore can't lend it to you.

....

可以的。

對不住，沒有多的了。

13. Alright.

Sorry, but there's no more.

....

sleep right away, I would imagine that I could feel little creatures crawling up my legs. I would tell myself, "Nonsense, Winborn, you dusted your sleeping bag." In the morning I would shake out the bag and a multitude of little dead bodies would rain down onto the floor.

After the war, I read about the devastating effects of DDT on the environment. I am sorry if I caused any birds in China to have soft-shelled eggs, but I wouldn't have given up that little olive-drab can for anything.

The Chinese expression for the telephone was *"ta tien hua,"* which might be translated as "great electric voice." A telephone was answered by saying, *"wei."* One day when I walked into our place in Nanping, Chico was at the telephone saying, *"Wei, wei, wei, wei. . . ."* I thought he had gone off his rocker. He was OK. It seems that the operator listening in on a call would disconnect it if the line went silent. Chico was simply keeping the line open while the party at the other end went to look for something.

The British Consulate, which had been evacuated to Nanping from Foochow when the Japanese took over, was a neighbor of ours. One time when I answered the telephone, the caller asked for *"Ying kuo lin se gwah"* which of course means British Consulate. I happened to know their number because it was posted on the wall near the telephone. So I said, "Call four-one-two."

"Shenma, shenma?" (What, what?)

I tried using the national language (*Peiping hua*), *"Tsu-ee-erh."*

"Shenma, shenma?"

Well, how about the singsong local dialect? I suggested *"Say-ay-nay."*

Hao, hao, hao." (Good, good, good.)

Once I had occasion to call SACO in Kienyang. Sometimes long distance calls worked. The operator who took the call, a male, asked, "And what is your secret telephone number?" Each subscriber had a secret telephone number. This dissuaded strangers from walking in off the street and running up big phone bills. I thought I remembered our secret number and said, *"Ee-ling-liu-ee."*

"No, no, no. That is the secret telephone number of the bank. Your secret telephone number is *Ee-liu-ling-ee."*

"All right," I said, *"Ee-liu-ling-ee."* The call went through.

The Chinese truly hated the Japanese, but this was no reason for refusing to do business with them if it were to one's advantage to do so. For example, twice weekly a little train would chuff out of Kunming for Hanoi on the narrow-gauge railway the French had built. At the Indochina border the Chinese crew would get off and go to a rest shelter. The Japanese crew would board the train and drive it down to Hanoi. The next day they would drive the train back to the border and the Chinese would bring it on to Kunming. Business was good.

The Chinese sugar we could get in Nanping was brownish, full of sand and little sticks, and wet. It fermented rapidly. Drying it would have required a profligate expenditure of scarce fuel. So we had Chinese friends buy Japanese sugar. It was clean, practically white, and almost dry.

Willie and I would spend some time between trips shopping on the street in Nanping. I saw a vase that attracted my attention at once. It was cylindrical, about four inches in diameter by eleven inches high, cut from some variegated stone reminiscent of jade. An artisan had carved an intricate base for it out of hardwood, stained in a dark brown with a reddish hue. As usual, the woodcarver had used green wood which would shrink over the next few years so that it would have to be reworked to maintain a fit. The piece of stone had been bored through all the way along its axis leaving a nice thick wall. The bottom was closed with plaster, so that it would have held water, for a while at least.

"Willie," I said, "I want that vase." We started a long negotiation with the merchant which ended with his acceptance of the price he had expected to get from the start.

I took the vase up the hill and proudly showed it to the fellows in our unit. Their reaction was just what I might have expected. Janasky started it off with, "Winborn, you have finally done it. You have found something that is absolutely worthless."

The other chimed in with, "It's too small to become an umbrella stand."

"Too big for a pencil stand."

"And it doesn't have a bell on one end, so it can't be used as a sewer tile."[2]

"Absolutely useless" stone vase. (Photo by Winborn)

Typical Chinese
water pipes. One
draw per loading.
(Photo by Winborn)

Ku bronze, early Chou
Dynasty
(1122–255 B.C.)
Rudimentary
decoration. Ceremonial
wine cup.
(Photo by Winborn)

The women in Nanping were very fine and always helpful. They tended to be flat-chested, with one notable exception—a merchant known as "The Body." Periodically word would be passed around that The Body was scheduling another shopping trip to Shanghai and would take orders. It was easy for the Chinese to make trips to Shanghai—just expensive. The traveler had to pay to cross the Chinese lines and pay to cross the Japanese lines and then repeat these payments in the reverse order on the return trip.

Countless items of merchandise were simply not available in wartime provincial China. Our supply line to the Western world was tenuous at best even when existent. It was comforting to know that we had free access to the lush metropolitan markets of Shanghai.

The Body was a welcome addition to the community.

The uses the Chinese found for bamboo were numerous.

Short bamboo poles were frazzled most of the way and used as torches in night parades. The skeletons of the dragons in dragon dances were fabricated of bamboo. Japanese restaurants give diners a spread of bamboo chopsticks still attached together. (Breaking off one's own chopsticks assures the diner that he is getting unused sticks. The Chinese find it adequate to rinse off their bamboo chopsticks and re-use them indefinitely.)

Large bamboo poles lashed together side by side made rafts. The forward end of each pole was bent upward. Fishermen would prod these rafts out into the river using bamboo poles; obliging cormorants lined up on the deck.

Lengths of bamboo cut so that two or more nodes were retained served as bottles. A hole in the top node was fitted with a pithy stopper, and openings were bashed through any intermediate nodes. The wine, or whatever was in the bottle, would make a "glug-glug" sound as it was poured out.

A spring in the mountains behind our compound in Nanping furnished good water for the town. It was conveyed by means of an above ground water main which happened to pass through our front yard. The main was made of large diameter bamboo lengths with ends fitted together so closely that they leaked only a little. Holes plugged with pithy stoppers were provided at intervals. Whenever our houseboy (or anyone else) wanted to draw water, he would remove a stopper and collect a bucket full. It was considered bad form not to replace the stopper promptly.

I rigged up an ingenious set of poles for my mosquito tent. Naturally, I used lengths of bamboo with joints made of pieces of steel tubing from a Japanese airplane.

Carrier coolies' yoyo poles were made of bamboo.

The harnesses used by coolies to drag the Min Kiang River "steamboats" up the rapids were made of braided split bamboo. The fuel for these ships was charcoal, brought aboard in woven split bamboo bags.

Bamboo was sometimes used for furniture, but for once another material, rattan, was superior.

Artificial legs (uncommon) and false teeth were made of bamboo.

Chinese artists still love to use bamboo leaves as the model for their still life paintings.

We even ate the stuff. Young bamboo shoots when split up were quite tender. We called this dish "lumber."

When my Jeep was first turned over to me, it was still wearing its winter split bamboo top and side curtains. This gave it a sort of thatched effect. When I had it reupholstered, the cushions were stuffed with bamboo shavings, perhaps the best material in the world for this use.

And then there were bamboo ash trays, back scratchers, baskets, fish traps, floor mats, letter openers, cores for radio coils, roofs, cups, dippers, door springs, sampan masts, sampan spars, scaffolding, fans, fences, slide rules, umbrellas.

Thinking back on it, one article that I never did see in China was a bamboo fishing pole.

Jeeps were essential, but they simply were not rugged enough for China duty. Of course, springs were always breaking. But cracks in miscellaneous structural members were more troublesome. My Jeep had a particular problem with the mount for its five-gallon auxiliary gas can. We kept devising jury-rigs, but even bamboo failed us this time.

We needed steel, but where in Southeast China could we find steel? Well, there was a place. One day, while Willie and I were driving in the extreme northern sector of my territory we came across a bombed out railroad with scraps of steel lying all over the place. We retrieved some nice pieces of one-quarter inch plate.

Now all we had to do was find a welder. The nearest one was in Changting, four hard days drive to the south. So the next time we went to Changting we looked up the welder and overcame our problem with the mount.

It was surely convenient having all sorts of facilities in our own neighborhood.

Once out in the field, I found that the financial picture had taken on a somewhat different light than that depicted by the finance officer back in Kunming. After the long trip on which we worked over the Tony, I wrote the following informal letter to my commanding officers:

"First of all, there is no objection on my part to the present system insofar as the relatively large expenditures are concerned. But to handle the many small items in compliance with regulations and instructions would simply consume more time for bookkeeping than can be allotted. For example, consider one day's experiences on the trip. It is impossible to carry the voucher sheet on your person, because any paper is ruined within an hour by sweat if not by rain. Consequently, the records are placed in a briefcase. The briefcase is placed within the A-bag[3] to protect it from rain. The A-bag and maybe a musette bag are wrapped in oil paper and lashed to the end of the coolie's pole. We start out with seven coolies furnished by the magistrate. We don't know their names or addresses, and frankly don't care. But we pay each of them a little something. Due to the hot weather, we have three changes of coolies that one day, all of them procured either by the magistrate or by our guard. Some of them work well, and we buy them cigarettes and cakes.

We ferry a river and give $400 CN to the boatman. We buy a dinner for our guard and for the clerk and myself. I pay for my own chow, but the clerk's chow is an allowable item. That night we ride in two canal sampans and ferry another river, dribbling out a little money each time. Now if we were to break out the financial records and get signatures, chops, and fingerprints each time we spent $100 CN, we should have little time left to do anything else.

"Well, it is fairly easy to doctor up the accounts a bit so that they show about the right amount for the total expenditure even if a lot of small items are adjusted accordingly. I have, however, personal scruples against signing financial documents that are not exactly correct. I do not want to make any money out of the account, and, likewise do not like to pay for a lot of allowable items out of my own pocket.

"What I should like to do is this. Carry along a petty cash pouch out of which small items are paid. Then enter the amount spent on a trip as 'Allowable traveling expenses on trip from Yunhwo to Pingyang.' I should gladly sign for this item and it will show exactly what was spent. I should like to know how the Finance Department would react to this suggestion."

No changes were made in our financial instructions.

No one in Kunming had any way of knowing the proper price for items out in the provinces. I have bought Pirate cigarettes in a village for $30 CN while they were selling for $160 CN in Changting. The voucher system simply didn't accommodate some types of financial transactions. For instance, one time I lost heavily in an all-night poker game (personal expense) and borrowed $50,000 CN from a friendly magistrate, giving him an IOU on the back of one of my Chinese calling cards. The borrowed money was tax collections, largely in ones, twos and threes. I couldn't begin to get it all in my little steel box. In fact, I had difficulty in cramming it into an A-bag. Later on I had more money wired to me from Nanping so that I could repay the magistrate.

There was good reason to doubt that any Adjutant General's personnel were going to fly nine hundred miles, ride a Jeep for three rough days, and then walk for a week just to check a coolie's thumb print. It appeared to be in order for me to devise an alternative procedure, under which I would make a note of the exact amount of cash on hand we had when we started out on a trip, and then keep a precise record of all personal expenditures. Upon returning from a trip, I would count the current cash on hand, account for all personal expenditures, and by difference find the legitimate travel expense. Then my faithful Willie would borrow a handful of fountain pens with various colors of ink, fill out a multiplicity of entries on a voucher sheet, showing mostly places where we had been. He would go down on the main street of Nanping, stop anyone who came along and get him to sign a name or leave a thumbprint by an entry. The bottom line would come out exactly right. Everything worked out just fine. All allowable travel expenses were reimbursed. No army funds were lost or stolen. I was given a commendation for keeping the best-looking set of vouchers turned in to the Kunming office.

Somebody brought a copy of a service newspaper (*Yank* or *Stars and Stripes*) out from Kunming. One of the articles was about the rugged duty being served by a detachment of marines at an isolated outpost. They had no refrigeration to cool their beer! Did that faze them? Not the United States Marine Corps! These ingenious lads cut the top out of a fifty-five gallon drum, filled it with aviation gasoline, and dropped in their beer bottles. Then they turned on the power-driven air compressor that had been issued to them for inflating their tires and bubbled air through the gasoline. Evaporation cooled the fuel and the beer came out at just the right temperature for quaffing.

We Southeast China types could only mourn for the beer that was rationed to us but had to be consumed by our colleagues in Kunming because the airlift out East was so tight. We thought about the struggle we had trying to keep our Jeeps running on pine gas and alcohol because there was no gasoline. We remembered the hours spent in the hot sun pumping up tires with a hand pump.

Then we thought again of those marines out on their South Seas island—the poor, benighted bastards!

---

[1] Once while I was in the pharmacist's office, two injured coolies were brought in. One had the side of his face bashed in. The other, apparently, had a broken back. It seems that a photographic P-38, trying to land on the strip, had its landing gear collapse on one side. Base officials called out a gang of coolies who managed to lift up the wing on the bad side and get the gear down. Then they got out a truck to tow the P-38 off the strip, so somebody else could use it. They tied a rope from the truck to the defective landing gear. When the truck pulled, the gear collapsed again, dropping the wing onto the two coolies. Kittle turned them over to Chinese authorities as soon as he could. Later on, Kittle took the aerial camera out of the junked P-38 and got some excellent photographs with it. On my next trip to Changting, I admired the photographs. Kittle gave me prints, which now hang on my office wall.

[2] I still cherish my distinctive stone vase.

[3] See Glossary.

10

TRIP TO THE INTERIOR:

SHANGKAO

Janasky was recalled to the States after a long exemplary tour of duty. This left me in the potentially uncomfortable position of being Senior Officer Present but not Commanding Officer. Major Slack in Kunming was still our commanding officer. Fortunately, all personnel in the Nanping unit—army and navy alike—were top notch and never gave me a hint of a problem.

Corporal Harold R. Featherstone, USA, whom I didn't know well at all, arrived in Nanping while I was away on a trip. A handsome, strapping young man, he seemed quite affable. Between trips, most of us would have some red-hot project under way—work on the Jeep, fuss with our travel gear, have some furniture made to order, go shopping, take a series of photographs—you name it. Featherstone would sit. If you asked him to do something, he would do just what you asked, willingly and promptly. Then he would sit again.

For once, the notice came through official channels. An enemy plane was down near Shangkao, Kiangsi Province, deep in the interior. The first report indicated that the crash site was inaccessible, in an area completely controlled by the Japanese. We radioed the AGFRTS post nearest the site requesting information, but didn't get through. I decided to take Willie and go on a Jeep trip to the Chinese Third War Zone Headquarters in Wutu seeking firmer intelligence. It seemed logical to add Featherstone to the party.

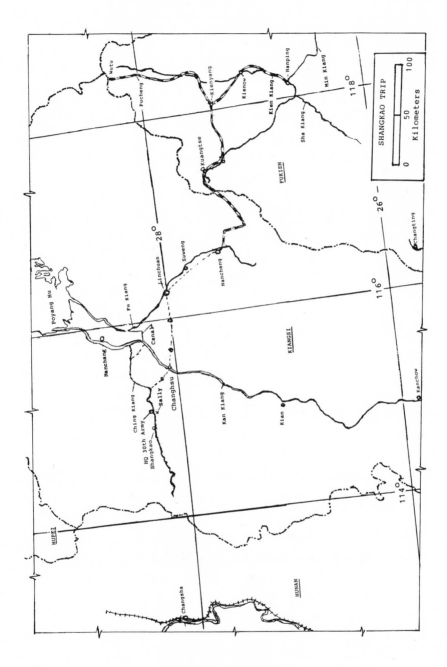

(Map by Byron Winborn)

We reached Kienyang in four hours and found a SACO officer who knew the territory around Shangkao. He told us that we could get through and gave us a list of places where we could spend the night. So we changed course ninety degrees and headed into the setting sun.

We stopped in Kuangtse at the German Catholic mission with its ramshackle cow shed out in back. This town had always been in Fukien Province but Kiangsi provincial troops got there first after the Japanese pulled out, so now it was in Kiangsi. Ethnologically, historically and geographically, Kuangtse belonged to Fukien. The two provinces squabbled over the issue from time to time. After seeing the place, I didn't feel inspired to fight very hard for its return to Fukien.

In the morning we found a tire down with a spike in it. Nobody around could repair it, so we put on the spare and continued on our way. We had moved out of the mountains of Fukien and, for once, the road was good, much like a back country dirt road in the States. When we were ten kilometers out of Nancheng, our destination for the day, another tire blew in a big way with a break that you could have put your foot through. The tire was ruined, so I just bounced on slowly. While doing so, I suffered the crushing humiliation of getting passed by a Chinese charcoal-burning truck. I was glad that I was over in the next province so that, hopefully, none of my friends would ever hear about it.

When we got to Nancheng, I sent a telegram to my gang in Nanping asking them to try to have another tire trucked up to me. I remembered that flats tended to come in groups of three, so I had a suspicious looking tire pulled off its rim just to see if there was anything wrong with it. There was, but a boot could be put behind the break in the casing. The Catholic mission at Nancheng was superb, with all Irish fathers except for one American. Sure and it was a pleasant time that we had there, lounging on the porch, sipping wine, and listening to tales of the gossoons in County Killarney.

We had arrived at the mission early in the afternoon. A group of us, including Willie, Featherstone, and some locals, set out to do the town. Just outside the gate we found a pretty little girl of eight or nine lying on the ground. She was crying softly. I stopped the party and sent one of the locals back to tell the priests about the child.

Several hours later we returned to the mission. The little girl was lying in the same place, only now she was dead. Flies were crawling on her face.

After Jimmy Doolittle's famous Tokyo raid in 1942, quite a number of his airmen parachuted into what later became the northern part of my territory. The Chinese had bravely and miraculously spirited all the Americans away to safe havens, far to the west. Then the Japanese had, belatedly, launched their retaliation campaign. I saw expanses of rubble where once important towns had been leveled. I stayed in some, like Lishui, which had been rebuilt with largely temporary construction.

The Catholic mission at Nancheng was in the midst of the retaliation region. The Irish fathers had many stories to tell, some trivial, some not.

This mission had beautiful oak furniture. A Japanese soldier used to come around of an evening, crawl onto a table, and aimlessly carve grooves into its top. A refined, well-educated major would carry on long, cultured conversations in English with one of the priests. The father spoke to him about the soldier who was carving up the mission's furniture. The major said, "Ah, yes. Every military organization has its undesirable element." The soldier would go right on hacking. As the major bade farewell one night, he reached out, plucked a fountain pen from the priest's breast pocket and stuck it in his own. A fine fountain pen was the most coveted status symbol of the era.

The father told me that, all in all, the Chinese fatalities in the retaliation numbered around three hundred thousand. General Chennault's estimate of these fatalities was two hundred and fifty thousand. I asked what the Chinese reaction to the Doolittle raid had been, once they learned how much it had cost them.

"They were overwhelmingly delighted," he replied, "to know that the Americans were finally coming to their aid in their prolonged war against the Japanese."

The road was impassable beyond Nancheng, so Willie chartered a boat for us on the Fu Kiang (also called Tung Kiang). When I saw the boat, I said, "Willie, surely you can do better than that." It turned out that no other boat around was any better. It was just a sample of the kind of country that we were moving into—flat, hot, dull and uninspired with people who answered to the same description. We wished we were back in Fukien or Chekiang.

There were supposed to be two boatmen, but one of them lit out, so we sort of oozed downstream in the blistering heat. With no roads, railways or industry, the atmosphere was crystal clear, and we broiled in the brutal sun, whose radiation was fiercer than anything I had known in the States. It could raise blisters in ten minutes and knock you flat on the ground if you were not very careful to hold your parasol at just the right angle.

It was dark when our boat reached Suweng and we put up at the Catholic mission there. The staff was all Chinese except for one foreigner, a most sociable American, who provided us with baths and loaned us his underwear while our skivvies were being washed. He was a firm believer in the therapeutic value of *bei kan jiu*. A cute nine-year-old girl at the mission attached herself to me and spent most of her time fanning me with youthful vigor. She was deeply concerned when I neglected to cross myself before eating.

The "wheel" of the town came around and invited us to be his guests at the Chinese opera that evening. It was already late and we were sleepy, but we accepted. Since we were the wheel's guests, we stalked down to the front row center, shooed the occupants out of their seats, and made ourselves comfortable. We cracked watermelon seeds, drank tea, and enjoyed the show, which was acted with great talent. With the help of the priest, and of Willie, I could follow the plot except when I dozed.

It was a double feature, and we missed most of the first show. The second was entitled "Who Has Got the Heads?" The first hero had a pal who was in jail and was now critically ill. The hero contacted a talented doctor who was too proud to enter a jail. The hero then slashed off two heads with a single stroke of his sword, apparently one of the heads inadvertently. It didn't seem to matter whose heads they were. The decapitation was staged so convincingly that I felt sure I could see blood spurting out. A second hero, also a friend of the man in jail, planted one of the heads in the doctor's office. The doctor was unduly squeamish about severed heads and tried to conceal it under his robe. This made the magistrate's men suspicious, so they arrested the doctor. The plot worked out so that the doctor would be released if he agreed to treat the prisoner. He did so with great repugnance, and the prisoner recovered immediately. This normally would have been the happy ending of the play.

But this night the cast improvised a special ending in honor of their distinguished guests, the corporal and me. The new ending centered around a sword dance which was truly spectacular. The swords had handles six feet long, looked like axes, and seemed to be heavy. Two actors fenced each other with the nonchalance of high school drum majorettes twirling batons. I stayed wide awake throughout the sword dance, waiting for the moment when a sword would come flying out and behead a few people in the orchestra section—which of course never happened.

Nevertheless, it was a memorable evening.

Tax collectors were called "publicans" in Roman times. The people of that era didn't like publicans at all. The people of China didn't like tax collectors either. The collectors not only frequently raised the tax rates, but also levied taxes in advance. They were collecting 1975 taxes when I was there in 1945.

All civilian officials had a corresponding military rank. In Suweng the tax collector had the rank equivalent to a major. During our brief stay there, someone shot the major and his wife. They were still alive when we shoved off the next morning. A couple of weeks later we passed through Suweng on our way back. I didn't think to ask if the major and his wife had survived. I suppose I knew the answer. Why in the world would a person go to any trouble to save the life of a tax collector in China?

The next day, after a mere five-hour cruise, our boat reached Linchuan, a major city with an imposing Catholic mission. It was run by a foreigner, an American who must have had a deep well, because his shower felt icy cold to us. Linchuan had once been served by several fine motor roads, but they had all been destroyed by the Chinese and no motor vehicles had been seen in the area for eight years.

We had to go overland for the next hitch, which was to be one hundred and eighty *li*—three days. As a concession to the heat, we ordered chairs, but I never used mine. Following a demolished motor road, we stripped down to shorts, socks, boots and a parasol, and looked forward only to the cool of the evening. Night would find us in some breathless oven of a room, tossing in puddles of our own sweat, yearning only for the morning when we could move on to somewhere else— anywhere.

We drank many quarts of hot tea, sweating profusely. We wouldn't have touched any iced drink even if, miraculously, one had been offered to us because we knew that in our overheated condition a cold drink would have brought on violent stomach cramps.

The third day turned out to be the worst yet. By 0830 we Americans very nearly had heat strokes, and we had to seek refuge in a magistrate's quarters, lying low until 1730 when we struck out again. The magistrate said that he would have horses sent out from Changhsu to bring us in the last twenty-five *li*. It turned out that all the horses in Changhsu had been evacuated. I told my party that we would lay over a day in the city and rest up.

As we approached the place, a police escort came out and greeted us, saying, "We have reserved a room for you in the best hotel in town." When we saw the room, our spirits drooped. It was another oven with two tiny, barred windows and it was noisy and dirty. We couldn't stand the hotel's stinking head, so we went aboard a sampan in the river and used theirs.

We had been back in the hotel only a few minutes when the police commissioner called on us. It seemed that the mayor had evacuated because the enemy were getting close, leaving the police commissioner as the acting wheel. He was a fine host who invited us first to the public baths. We strode through the lobby of the best hotel in town and down the main street clad only in skivvy shorts and sandals. The baths were refreshing, with boys to scrub us all over, easy chairs, and punkahs.

After the baths, the commissioner took us out for dinner at an open air restaurant on the banks of the Kan Kiang. There was a delightful little breeze. The food was excellent and the wine surprisingly good. It was 0100 the next morning by the time we got back to the hotel, dog tired but quite content with the world for the moment. We tumbled into our sacks and fell asleep immediately. Ten minutes later I sprang up, being eaten alive. Never again did I neglect to use that little olive drab can of army insecticide.

We were now to ferry across the Kan Kiang and head for Shangkao to the north and west. Three days before, someone had told me that this trip would be one hundred and eighty *li*. It scaled one hundred and fifty *li* on a crude local map, and since the countryside was supposed to be flat, one hundred and eighty *li* seemed plausible. We knew that Shangkao was on the Ching Kiang, which flowed into the Kan Kiang up in Japanese country a little north of where we were, but we hoped to be able to cruise on it farther upstream.

Some of the magistrate's male secretaries were still in town. We had them call in the head of the coolies' labor union and certain other travel experts to find out which trails we should take. One of the experts said, "Shangkao is two hundred *li* west of here." Two others were certain it was one hundred and twenty *li*. One insisted, "No, no, no. It is only ninety *li*."

I asked, "Would it be possible for us to go part way by sampan on the Ching Kiang?"

"We have never heard of such a river."

"There is no such river."

After conferring for four hours, their opinions jelled to the point that they were able to plot a route for us. It would be one hundred and fifty *li*. I then asked, "Could we travel by night so as to stay out of the sunlight?" One expert immediately said, "Yes, the coolies prefer to go by night." The head of the coolies' union said, "Impossible."

We strung along with the man who had said yes. The experts conferred for another full hour, and finally reached a verdict. "Yes, you can travel by night. But if you do, you will have to take the shorter route, one hundred and thirty-five *li*, because the trail is better and it doesn't go through the mountains."

It could have happened only in China.

We decided to get chairs to spare ourselves a bit. There were no chairs in Changhsu—they had all been evacuated. So we had some bamboo litters made for $100 CN apiece—overpriced. We ferried across the Kan Kiang just as darkness fell. Since no chair coolies were available, we hired carrier coolies who had a much rougher gait. The litters were saggy and extremely uncomfortable, but we were far too tired to walk much of the way. The vertebrae in my neck and between my shoulder blades ached for days.

Forty *li* out we got down from the litters to ferry a stream. Willie asked the local coolies, "Is there a river going to Shangkao?"

"Yes, yes. It is only thirty *li* from here."

We had a couple of hours delay while Willie rounded up a fresh supply of coolies.

We got to the nonexistent river before noon. After much *hua-la hua-la,* Willie succeeded in hiring a two-man fishing sampan. The little fish taken that morning had been laid out on the woven split-bamboo canopy to dry in the sun. That evening one of the fishermen dumped the catch (all that the flies had left) into the rice and there was our supper. Cultured by all those millennia of civilization, he had scaled the fish. A few more millennia and he might have been cultured to the point of eviscerating them.

As we were poled into the dusk, we heard a loud *"Nah gah!"* A Chinese sentry was challenging us from the bank. Oh, just another inspection station. As was our custom, we shouted *"Mei kuo ren"* (American) and moved blithely on our way. This time it didn't take. The sentry repeated his challenge in tones we could hardly ignore, especially since he said that he would shoot if we didn't come in to the bank. Willie said that he meant it. We landed and showed ourselves to the sentry and still he was not satisfied. He called up the bank for one of his superiors to come down. The superior called down his superior and soon we were talking to real brass without any success at all. So I clambered up the river bank with my credentials in hand looking for the inspection station itself. Clearing the crest I found myself in the oasis we had longed for all of these days—a veritable Garden of Eden with trees, shrubbery, and clean new buildings with windows. It was the headquarters of a Chinese army. I turned my papers over to a colonel and he turned them over to the general and at last I was accepted as an ally and a gentleman. Of course, we must stay there that night and, of course, we must be the general's guests for a big banquet. Of course!

The military situation in this sector was that a large Japanese garrison occupied Nanchang, a city about thirty-five kilometers north of the point at which my party had crossed Kan Kiang and headed west. Japanese forces that had made the drive on Kanchow in December, 1944, were now trying to withdraw to the north. Fierce resistance by a Chinese army had stalled them at Kian, which was four hours by powerboat south of the point at which we had crossed the Kan Kiang. Some other Japanese, stationed at Changsha to the west of us, were trying to move eastward to relieve their comrades at Kian. A second Chinese army, the Thirtieth, was resisting the Changsha army, letting it advance slowly but inflicting heavy casualties on it. My host was Commanding General of the Thirtieth. We were close enough to the battlefield to hear the rumble of artillery fire in the distance.

Now that the general knew what our mission was, he told us that while the wreckage of the plane we were after had been taken to Shangkao, the place where the plane had crashed was across the river from us, not far upstream. He added, "The airplane had three heads, two large feet, and one small foot. It broke into pieces up in the sky during a storm. One officer and four enlisted men were aboard, and they were all killed. What model was it?"

Dinner was elaborate, and midnight slipped by before it was ready. Proper etiquette would demand that the general and I share many, many toasts of *bei kan jiu,* the devastating rice brandy, each toast culminating in *"kan pei,"* meaning "dry glass." The general was in the middle of a heavy battle and I was in the middle of a wearing trip. Neither of us wanted to confound his situation with a *bei kan jiu* hangover, with which we were only too familiar. Some way or other, we very neatly negotiated a tacit understanding. A special colonel was trotted out to drink *kan peis* with the distinguished Americans. It became evident that this colonel was a mighty powerful man with the *kan pei.* My man, Featherstone, took it upon himself to uphold the honor of America. Perhaps I had underrated the lad a bit. The general politely *sui-bienned* the toasts. I strung along with him.

The colonel was good, and I give him credit. He proposed toast after toast and the *kan peis* rang through the night like so many echoes chasing each other. Featherstone was right with him drink for drink. The pace began to tell on the colonel. He slipped the high sign to the waiter and from then on his glass was filled only part way. He would drink and his glass would still be part full. Featherstone deigned not to notice these little irregularities. His glass would runneth over and he would drain it to the last drop. The colonel began explaining how much more he could have taken in his prime, some twenty years ago. The corporal gave no quarter. Now, minutes would elapse before the colonel screwed up his courage for the next toast. The corporal stayed right with him. Finally, after a long pause the colonel came up with what had to be the finale for the night, "With the help of the Fourteenth Air Force, China is going to win this war against Japan!"

It was then that the corporal delivered his coup de grace. He responded immediately with an even more magnificent toast of his own, "China is going to conquer the Japanese people and rule their country for a thousand years."

The colonel gulped this one down and excused himself. He mumbled something about not feeling well as he stumbled out of doors.

Featherstone beckoned the waiter over, pushed out his glass and said, "Gimme a nightcap to settle my stomach."

A commander can grow mighty fond of his troops.

The next morning we were guided to the area across the river where the fragments of the airplane had come to earth. One engine had made a gouge in the ground way over there. The other engine had impacted off in a different direction. Wreckage of the fuselage, wing and tail had been scattered all over the place. Every bit had been picked up and taken to Shangkao.

A little mound marked the shallow grave in which the crew had been buried. One of the local Chinese had Willie explain to me, "The

Double trouble with tires. On the road between Wutu and Kienyang, with two flats and no spare. (Photo by Willie)

At noon along the trail one day we stopped at a farmhouse for lunch. An old sow was in the yard. Her belly dragged in the dust. Willie said that all she ate was rice gruel, and that it was not an adequate diet. I wanted to take her picture, but she was shy and ran into the house where she lived. So I paid for a bowl of gruel to entice her out again, and took her portrait. (Photo by Winborn)

people in this area are very poor. Of necessity, we took all of the clothing and boots."

I picked up an officer's garrison cap with its red army star, which had lain on top of the mound, right in the middle of the site. Willie admonished me, "Dead men's hats are not worn."

"OK," I replied, "I'll just cut off the star for a little souvenir." I put the star with my papers. A few days later I noticed that it had disappeared. I suspect that, once again, my faithful Christian Willie had saved me from demons.

We were about to leave when someone said, "You know, that airplane carried thousands of needles."

"Good," I said, "give me one to send in as a sample."

Nobody had any idea what had happened to all the needles. Finally, after much negotiation, I offered to pay. Immediately someone said, "Oh, I think I can get you one."

It turned out to be a very large hypodermic needle. Willie could read the tiny characters inscribed on it, because they were Chinese ideographs, which comprised one of the systems used by the Japanese. He said, "This needle is for horses."

Do you suppose that for want of needles, horses were lost; for want of horses, battles were lost; for want of victories . . .?

For our trip to Shangkao, the Chinese Army got us a pretty fair sampan with two boatmen. Just as we boarded it early in the evening, a terrific storm blew up. The little river was whipped into whitecaps. I said, "Let's shove off and have some sport with the waves." The boatman answered, "Oh, no. We must stay tied up here until the storm blows itself out." When it did, we cruised for the rest of that night, all of the next day, and finally reached Shangkao at 0230 the following morning.

Yi Ting Lo, the magistrate of Shangkao and a retired professor, was obviously a cultured gentleman who spoke some English. He had sent us a radiogram saying, "DO NOT COME. JAPANESE CLOSING IN RAPIDLY." We never received it.

Professor Yi showed us the wreckage, which was in pieces small enough to be lugged in by coolies. It had been a Sally, a two-engine heavy bomber. It was several years old and had only limited intelligence significance, but it had carried a code book, the diary of a soldier who had recently returned from Okinawa, a radar, the airplane's log books, and other pertinent documents, all of which had been taken to the headquarters of the Chinese Third War Zone at Wutu.

As we worked hard processing the wreckage, we could hear the field pieces thudding away. The magistrate did not sleep a wink that night—he was on the telephone every minute, and, since we shared his quarters, we didn't sleep much either.

The next morning the battle zone was obviously moving in closer, and the artillery fire sounded pretty damned loud. A courier came in and reported that a Chinese captain had just been killed in the battle. Everyone commented on the fact that the captain and I had the same rank.

We had our boatmen keep their sampan moored on the Shangkao waterfront until we were ready to make a fast getaway. How did we do this? We simply withheld their pay until we were ready to go. Professor Yi was having conniptions worrying over the possibility that the Japanese might capture or kill us in his territory. He didn't conceal his relief when we finally shoved off and left him free to evacuate.

Two *li* out of Shangkao, while the noise of artillery fire was still loud, we came to a seven-story pagoda on the south bank of the river. I wanted to find out if we could see any smoke or flame from seven stories up, so I ordered the sampan into the bank. We entered the pagoda and climbed up to the top level. It was constructed of very skillfully cut and fitted stone masonry. A neat stairway ran from each level up to the next. I exclaimed, "Willie, this pagoda is most impressive. How old is it?"

"Not old. Eight hundred years."

We cruised down the Ching Kiang for two and one half days, eating and sleeping on the sampan. It was during this interval that a Japanese airplane flew over, low and very close, probably reconnoitering the headquarters of the Chinese Thirtieth Army.

My party of three, plus the two sampan fishermen, couldn't quite see it over the crest of the river bank. We could hear it circling around for a second pass.

I told Willie, "Hand me my carbine." Using the traditional technique for shooting down enemy planes from fishing sampans, I laid on my

Our trusty sampan and its crew. (Photos by Winborn)

Old stone pagoda a few *li* downstream of Shangkao. We could hear cannon fire up-river. I decided to stop the sampan, climb the pagoda, and find out whether we could see the muzzle blasts. We couldn't because there was high ground in between.

From top of pagoda looking down at our sampan

Looking up-river
toward Shangkao

Looking south

back on the deck with the butt of the carbine stock pressed firmly against my shoulder and with the muzzle pointed into the sky. Admittedly it was a long shot that I could put a slug into a vital spot such as an oil cooler, but it was worth the old try. I could visualize the headlines: "Navy Lieutenant in Command of Tiny Sampan Shoots Down Jap Aircraft." We heard the plane come closer and closer and finally blasting past without quite coming into sight. It did not return.

Everywhere we went the people said the Japanese were forty *li* away. No, it was twenty *li*. The towns were all dirty, grubby places you could smell five *li* away. In some of them, the people had never seen Americans before. The area had been devastated by the Japanese during the retaliation, and we saw many acres of rubble where sizable towns had once been located. We reached a point at which we decided that it wouldn't be advisable to follow the river any closer to the enemy garrison at Nanchang. We gave up our sampan and struck out on a long forty *li* walk to a village on the banks of the Kan Kiang, considerably upstream from where we had crossed it on the way west. The trail was miserable and there was heavy rain, but rain was better than that sunshine. The magistrate was most friendly. He had a telephone that rang all night and a plentiful supply of bedbugs.

In the morning we awoke to a scene of unimaginable confusion. Japanese troops to the south were moving again and might sweep into our village at any moment. Everybody was fleeing with whatever goods they could carry. The rich had hired the available coolies to tote out their wealth, mostly in the form of big rolls of silk. People were running away in every direction, including straight toward the approaching army.

We knew that the Fu Kiang, on which the string of Catholic missions was located, lay to the east of us. A canal system interconnected the Kan Kiang and the Fu. I asked Willie, "In which direction does the water in the canal flow?"

"In both directions."

"Impossible!"

Willie was right. A system of floodgates had been installed by some ancient emperor. By opening or closing gates upstream or downstream on one river or the other, the water could be made to flow in either direction.

In spite of the uproar, Willie managed to commandeer a small canal sampan, but he couldn't find sampan crewmen anywhere. He finally drafted two land carrier coolies and we headed east on the canal. Our coolies turned out to be hopelessly inept at poling a sampan. We would broach into one bank, then the other. We were not getting away from that place nearly as fast as the Japanese surely were approaching it. I had to accept loss of face and take over the bow pole. It was indeed tricky to handle. After quite a while, I got the knack of using it. I then trained the bow coolie, who learned surprisingly well. Next I took over the stern pole, which had an entirely different feel. I finally mastered the art of handling it and trained the stern coolie, who also learned well. We now began to glide along right smartly.

Late in the afternoon, we reached one of the ancient emperor's flood gates. We had to portage around it. Our little sampan was heavier than we and the crew could lift. A strangely assorted gang of local people pitched in to give us a hand. While they sang an ancient chant and everyone strained to his utmost, we got that sampan over the embankment. "How wonderful," I thought. "What a heartening example of Allied cooperation." Then the patriarch of the local people came around and asked me for money.

Dinner was something we had on lucky days. This was not a lucky day. It soon got dark. I was very tired and dropped into a deep sleep.

I awoke with a start. The night was pitch black. Our sampan was moving well. I looked at my watch—midnight. I looked at a wrist compass that I wore—we were headed straight north! Were we about to hear a loud "*Dah ree gah!*" as an enemy sentry challenged us?

I asked Willie, "Does anyone aboard have any idea where we are?" Nobody did.

"Willie, tell the senior boatman to go ashore, wake up a farmer, and find out if we are still in clear territory."

The boatman came back and reported that it was all right—there was one last Chinese outpost a few *li* ahead of us. Waking up to find my team moving in pitch darkness straight into an area controlled by the enemy, where one of their sentries might challenge us at any moment gave me a sensation I never forgot.

At 0230 our sampan nosed into the outpost, which was at the confluence of the canal with the Fu Kiang. The sentry let us tie up to his dock, but he was not inclined to wake up anyone else in his outfit. When the others finally did get up, they invited us in to have a little rice for breakfast.

We found that the local magistrate had evacuated to the outpost and I showed him my papers. Reading them, he said, "Oh, you are attached to the Fourteenth Air Force." So he gave me a detailed map of Nanchang, which pinpointed the location of the quarters of each Japanese officer, giving his name and rank. The magistrate asked me to have the Fourteenth fly over and bomb and strafe their quarters. Army personnel the world over seem to fancy having enemy positions reduced the easy way—let the air arm do it.

The Chinese at the outpost got us a pretty fair sampan on the Fu Kiang, with an enterprising youth as the skipper and his younger brother as assistant. The brother had a severe case of trachoma, and had to keep washing his rotting eye with river water.

We were on this sampan two and one-half days, making good one hundred and fifty *li* upstream. In Chekiang Province we had made considerably better time against a swifter current. We reached Linchuan by noon, and, to our surprise, the boatmen pulled into the bank and stopped.

"What's wrong?"

"We can't take you any farther."

"Why not? The river goes in the right direction much farther."

"We would be more than a hundred *li* from home and our mother would worry about us."

"I am ten thousand *li* (actually it was more like forty thousand) from my home and my mother worries about me, but I have to keep on going until we have driven the Japanese out of your country."

Even Willie couldn't negotiate this one, and since it was too late in the day to start making travel plans, we called on our Catholic missionary friend. Traveling part of the time on horseback, and part on foot, spending one night with a magistrate, we got back to Nancheng and our Irish friends. Miraculously a tire had come in for us, so we could drive again. Generally, a day's trip in a Jeep would cover about five times as much ground as a day's walk, but on those roads the ride was more tiring.

Deciding that I really should share part of the glory of it all, I let Featherstone drive. Willie sat in the middle and I took the right seat. While we were still in the flat country of Kiangsi, the road was so good that the corporal got us up to a searing thirty-five miles per hour. Suddenly he swerved sharply to the left and then immediately back again without quite rolling the Jeep over. He said, "Did you see that big old snake? I got the last four feet of his tail."

Pretty soon we were back on the curving mountain roads of Fukien. Guard rails were unheard of because, after all, the farmers needed all the firewood they could get. We were all stripped to the waist. A large grasshopper flew in and landed on the middle of Featherstone's chest. The corporal looked down and tried to come in from behind and grab it. The grasshopper shifted position. Featherstone came in from the new angle. The grasshopper shifted again. The mountain road started swerving to the left. A high embankment rose on that side. A stone retaining wall flush with the road was on the right. Some shrubs were beyond the wall. The Jeep kept going straight until it was almost off the right side of the road. It was too late to yell at Featherstone and give him time to react.

I reached over Willie and threw the wheel hard to the left. We slammed into the embankment in a cloud of dust, stalling the engine. We got out and looked at the shrubs on the right side of the road. They turned out to be the tops of bamboo trees forty-five feet tall.

The grasshopper had made a fast exit. Nobody said a word. The Jeep started and we were on our way again. Ten minutes later, I said, "OK, Featherstone, it's my turn to drive."

As I recall, my turn took us all the way back to Nanping.

We stopped over with SACO in Kienyang. I was accustomed to getting up early so that we could walk as far as possible before the heat really clamped down. I woke at 0400 and turned on a little radio that happened to be in the dormitory. Armed Forces Radio came on the air and announced that the US Air Force had just dropped a secret superbomb on a Japanese town called Hiroshima. The bomb was more destructive than some unbelievable number of tons of TNT.

We all knew that the enemy had started pulling back toward its homeland, and we supposed that the war would end with a gigantic assault against the Japanese islands in 1946. This invasion would have been horribly bloody for both sides. The TAI units would have been pulled into the middle of the fray along with the combat units. Would the appearance of this superbomb shorten the War?

It was two hours before anyone else woke up so that I could even talk about it. When one is traveling hard on detached duty, it is important to keep fit—eat regularly and get a good night's sleep. Of course it was perfectly clear what each of us had to do—just carry on until he received new orders.

We drove up north to the Chinese headquarters in Wutu to request that the documents from the Sally be made available to a TAI Japanese interpreter at some accessible location. We put up at Rosholt's AGFRTS outpost and spent the night there. The next day we called on a general who insisted that I make my request in writing, so I borrowed a typewriter.

A young official of the US Department of State contacted us. He wanted to go south. His rather unusual vehicle for traveling in China was a trailer. We hooked it on to my Jeep. All of this took most of the day, so we stayed over a second night and took off the next morning. We were barely underway when one of our tires went flat. It was always much harder than it should have been to pull a Jeep tire off the rim and remount it, so we took the tire back to a good mechanic in Wutu who was handy at this job. We finally headed south again, planning to spend the night in Kienyang.

A few hours out two tires on my Jeep went flat simultaneously. No one in the area could repair them. With only one spare, this situation normally would have slowed down the war effort drastically. As it was, I simply borrowed a tire from my passenger's trailer. Willie and I left the State Department official and Featherstone to guard the trailer while we went back to Wutu. The borrowed tire was one of those made by using one-quarter-inch carriage bolts to fasten together good sections of tires that had blown out in their bad sections. It wasn't a high speed tire. The good mechanic repaired both flats and Willie and I returned to our companions. All of this consumed a good many hours, but now we were on our way again.

Not much later, darkness caught up with us. A couple of hours into the night, the Jeep stopped running with an acute electrical problem. Breaking out flashlights, we began searching for whatever was wrong. While this was going on, some local Chinese soldiers kept coming around asking anxiously "When are you going to move on?" We couldn't understand why they were so agitated. In the extreme southern part of the territory there was a remote possibility that a tiger might come around at night, but certainly not this far north. We finally learned what the soldiers were so concerned about—"*tu fei.*" *Ah, tu fei*! Bandits might be after us.

Some way or other we corrected our electrical problem, which turned out to be an intermittent short. We still had enough battery left to get started, so we drove on through the night, reaching Kienyang at about 0400 hours. We were considerate enough not to wake up the navy, but kept going until we got back to Nanping in the middle of the morning. We relaxed and got a little something to eat for the first time in more than twenty-four hours. That night we slept in our own beds. The next night, for the first time in twenty-seven nights, we went to bed in the same place where we had started out the day.

11

TOURISTS IN FOOCHOW

AND A

RESCUE TRIP

By early August, 1945, our TAI unit in Nanping was operating almost too smoothly. Mail was coming into Changting nearly every week. We were finally able to get urgently needed technical supplies. The unit now had a skilled photographer and a Nisei for translating Japanese. The Japanese were pulling out of South China, so our military threat was vanishing. Pretty soon we might not even have to go out and work over their downed airplanes. The Chinese were assisting us by putting up road signs in English that read: "Alarming!"

Then the Bomb was dropped. A matter of days later, our radio picked up an Armed Forces broadcast saying "Japan has surrendered!" We started a big celebration. Everyone broke out his one little jar or can of stateside goodies and his one bottle of stateside liquor. We fired our weapons into the sky and, as usual, the mayor pulled a *jing bao* so he could turn off the lights in town without losing face. Just when the festivities were really warming up, our radio told us that the report had been erroneous—no surrender yet. We collapsed. End of party. When the real surrender came four days later, we barely reacted.

Everything stopped. No more airplanes. No more mail. No radio messages. Then after two weeks, a British radioman handed me a penciled copy of a message he had intercepted. It was addressed to me by a naval lieutenant, Lasley, in Kunming: "MAKE A SURVEY OF

The Japanese finally surrendered and I no longer thought about them hearing my Rolls razor. (Photo by Bellew)

With the war over, with no instructions as to what to do next, and with a good supply of hand grenades and quarter-pound TNT packets, we decided to go fishing in the river near Nanping. We brought along a Japanese inflatable boat to retrieve our harvest. If we threw the hand grenade as soon as it was armed, or the can of TNT as soon as the fuse was lit, they would sink too far beneath the surface of the river before detonating. In the photo at the right the explosive sank too deep before detonating. (Photos by Winborn)

We would hold the active explosive above our shoulders a second or two before throwing. Timed just right.

From left to right: Yamamura, Featherstone, Bellew, Sammy (interpreter), Winborn, Burton, Peppler, four unidentified fish. (Photo by Willie)

THE CONDITION OF ROADS TO SHANGHAI AND THE CONDITION OF ROADS TO CANTON. REPORT FINDINGS TO ME." It also said, "STAND BY IN NANPING FOR FURTHER INSTRUCTIONS." It dawned on me that maybe I was no longer attached to the Fourteenth Air Force.

I had kept myself apprised of the condition of all area roads, most of which had been obliterated by the Chinese. Canton—no way. Shanghai—well, there was a road but it had a bottleneck at a ferry that was now holding up several weeks' worth of traffic. I was not about to stumble into a mess like that. So I immediately sent a message to Lasley, "THERE ARE NO ROADS NANPING TO CANTON" followed by one advising of the serious delay on the route to Shanghai.

We all had been on detached duty far too long to let someone twelve hundred miles away boss us around, so our whole TAI unit boarded the next Min Kiang "steamboat" and cruised down to the big city of Foochow for an outing. We stayed at what had once been the American Consulate there. The Japanese had used it as their headquarters during their long occupation. The last night they were in town they piled all their records in a big heap in the back yard and set them on fire. Then they all got drunk. They shoved off the next morning with hangovers. Lucas moved in right after they left. He found that the fire had gone out while most of the records were still legible. These included detailed reports on each of us—what mission we were on and where we were each night. It was belittling to know that we had not been considered worth chasing. We would have been mighty slippery to catch. Of course if they had caught one of us, the Fourteenth would have stopped bombing ships off the coast long enough to blast their headquarters. I suppose that the overall situation was belittling for them too.

Our party constituted what might be called the first group of tourists to visit Foochow after the long, dreary Japanese occupation. The merchants were delighted to see potential customers and brought out merchandise that had been stashed away for years. They offered us very attractive prices on fine lacquer ware and cloisonne. As we boarded the "steamboat" for the return trip upriver, we decided that maybe we were going to like this peacetime business.

Stranded in Nanping after Japan surrendered, the TAI fellows decided that it was an ideal time for an outing in the great city of Foochow. We booked passages on the next Min River "Steamboat." With the Japanese gone, the boats went all the way to Foochow itself, instead of cruising only to Mintsing. Following are photographs of the trip taken by Bellew. One of the Min River Transportation Company's fleet, taken from a sister ship cruising in the opposite direction.

A village on the shores of the Min Kiang.

Americans lolling on the sun deck of their luxury liner.

Going upstream was much slower. Our big boat needed help from trackers to traverse a stretch like this.

Bellew, Winborn, and Peppler with their ricksha coolies.

A main street in downtown Foochow. The dome at the left was said to be to protect a machine gun from passers-by.

Foochow from a watch tower in the city wall.

The American Consulate in Foochow. The Japanese used it as their headquarters while they had a garrison in Foochow. Lucas, the Old China Hand from Nanping, moved in when the Japanese bugged out. Everything was in good shape. We stayed there during our visit, unrolling our sleeping bags on the deck.

Ancient stone bridge across the Min Kiang near Foochow, bombed out during the war. Each horizontal stone beam weighed many tons. Nothing that the Chinese couldn't handle.

Sampans on the river near Foochow.

At dinner time on the day we got back to Nanping, SACO in Kienyang called me and said, "One of our planes is down—an R4D. It crashed near Shahsien (a town south of Nanping). We can't order you to do anything, of course, since you're not in SACO, but you are the naval officer nearest to the crash site. We'll surely appreciate whatever you can do for any possible survivors."

"I'll get volunteers and set out at once."

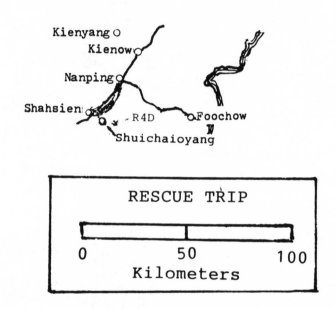

(Map by Byron Winborn)

Bellew and Yamamura volunteered immediately, and of course Willie joined us. We fired up my Jeep and roared out into the night. At one point the telephone wire going south had drooped across the road at just the height of a Jeep driver's neck. I noticed it in time. We tied a white rag to it as a warning to anyone coming along, particularly since the next travelers would probably be us coming back the next afternoon.

Some fifty-seven kilometers out we came upon six Chinese soldiers walking toward us. They told us, "We are on our way to the crash site. You have already driven past the place where the trail takes off eastward into the jungle."

We turned around and told the soldiers, "Climb aboard." They sat mostly on the hood of my ten-passenger Jeep, and, of course, completely blocked my vision. I told the soldier directly in front of me. "Please go back and sit on the right rear fender." A few kilometers farther on there was much yelling, so I stopped the Jeep. The soldier back there had fallen off into the road. Then I remembered, shamefacedly, that Jeeps don't have rear fenders. The poor soldier had hung on, sitting on thin air, until his arms gave out and then let go. He was scuffed up quite a bit, but nothing serious. We said, "Come on back aboard. We'll find space for you someway."

He replied, "No, thanks. I'll walk the rest of the way."

We parked the Jeep at the entrance to the trail and plunged into the jungle. At dawn, after walking thirty *li*, we came to a village called Shuichiaoyang. *Shui* means water, but we didn't see any water around there or any roads.

The official in the village told us, "The airplane crashed on the level top of a nearby mountain. A team has gone out to survey the situation. We suggest it would better for you to wait here until the team comes back and lets you know what may be needed." This made sense. The village had no food for us, but it did have clean mats on the floor on which we would take naps. Part of the team came back in an hour and reported that there were no signs of any personnel in or around the crash. Supposedly everyone aboard had bailed out.

My party started up the mountain. I was tired and it was twenty *li* up to the crash site. Willie was feeling fine and was the better part of a *li* ahead of me by the time he reached the top. Due to some acoustic peculiarity of the spot, Willie and I could carry on a conversation over that distance in just above our normal tones. Willie said, "There is plenty of food up here aboard the wreck—emergency rations. Come on up and eat." By the time I got up there, the Chinese had eaten everything except the cheese, which Chinese don't eat. So guess what I had for breakfast.

The airplane had done a commendable job of landing itself, completely out of fuel. The fuselage had remained in what appeared to be a survivable condition. The wings had snagged trees on each side, and both engines, with their propellers, had carried away and skidded a couple hundred feet ahead of everything else.

We gathered up all personal items, mostly pictures of girlfriends, some of them pretty cute. We then built a bonfire, dismounted the radar, and threw it and all classified manuals and documents into the fire. Salvage was out of the question, so I told the locals to have at it. They began cutting out aluminum for dishpans and replenishing their inventories of miscellaneous hardware.

We came down off the mountain and began our walk back through the jungle. At one point we noticed petroleum seeping out of the ground. (Geologists, please take note.) The Jeep started and we drove back to Nanping in time for dinner.

On the way back, we realized what a nightmare we might have gotten into. Suppose that there had been five critically injured Americans on top of that mountain. We could have hired local people to make litters and gently carry them down the mountain to shelter in Shuichiaoyang, which was a clean, friendly hamlet. But food there was so scarce that they had been unable to find any for us, even though we gladly would have paid for it. There was no doctor, no telephone, and no radio.

I would have had to send one of our party out for help, and that one would have been Bellew. Most Chinese felt a bitter hatred against all Japanese, including the American born. The fact that Nisei were accepted as members of the Armed Services of the United States, while the Chinese attached to American units were relegated to the status of civilian employees, aroused virulent jealousy. If I had let Yamamura out of our presence it would have been at the risk of his life. Bellew could have handled his assignment most competently. A couple of the Chinese soldiers could have accompanied him on the thirty *li* walk back to the Jeep. But they were not interpreters, and I could not spare Willie. Although the nearest telephone was in Shahsien, it was very unlikely that anyone there spoke English; so I would have instructed Bellew to drive all the way back to Nanping to round up more help, medical supplies, and badly needed food. Only then could the evacuation have been started.

We had many reasons to be delighted when we learned that all of the airmen had bailed out successfully and then had gone down to Foochow for a few days in the big city. They had a fine outing while we struggled to rescue them, but we didn't begrudge them one minute of it.

Bellew found a ricksha right in Nanping.

12

FAREWELL TO
SOUTHEAST CHINA:
HELLO SHANGHAI

After we got back to Nanping, the British radioman handed me a message from Lieutenant Ellis: "TAKE ALL PERSONNEL (9) AND ALL MATERIEL TO CHANGTING. TURN ALL JEEPS (3), TRAILERS (2) AND ALL MILITARY EQUIPMENT OVER TO THE COMMANDING OFFICER, CHANGTING AFB, AND GET A RECEIPT. PUT ALL PERSONNEL AND ALL INTELLIGENCE EQUIPMENT ABOARD A C-47 FOR KUNMING, WHICH WILL ARRIVE AT AN EARLY DATE."

We left Willie behind, and a big part of my bond to China just didn't exist any more.

Despite being delayed for a day in Yungan because there was rain in the mountains, we got to Changting before the C-47 did. When I asked Major Bull to give me a receipt for all the material I was turning in, he said, "Hell, boy, if you want a receipt write one yourself. I'll sign the goddamned thing.

The transport came in. Our party included two more men than it could carry, along with our gear. Maybe they didn't overload airplanes so much now that it was peacetime. Yamamura and I volunteered to wait over for the next one. No more airplanes came in. The radio in Changting had been dismantled, so I had no means of communication. Finally I got a long distance telephone call from the British radioman,

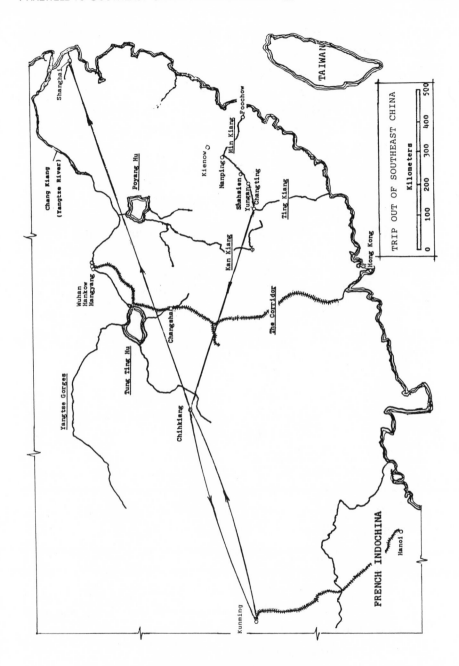

Trip Out of Southeast China
(Map by Byron Winborn)

who was still back in Nanping. The Chinese did not use insulators on their telephone lines, and to carry on a conversation over this distance was a monumental challenge. The two of us yelled at the top of our lungs. The radioman had picked up another message for me from Lieutenant Ellis: "REPOSSESS A JEEP, TAKE THE NISEI, AND DRIVE TO KIENOW. A NAVY R4D WILL PICK YOU UP THERE IN TEN DAYS."

I was not at all thrilled over the idea of driving all the way back to Kienow in peacetime. I had been there many times. Besides, it didn't seem any more likely that an airplane would come in there than where I was already. I decided that I had not heard that telephone call at all well. Sure enough, the next day a Chinese transport came into Changting. It had plenty of capacity to lift us out. We said goodbye to the gang at the base and boarded the plane. The pilot took off, circled once to gain altitude, and then headed west. I looked out the window at the green mountains and terraced rice paddies. That was the last time I saw Southeast China.

The Chinese airplane lifted us to Chihkiang, where I encountered a British agent. We were both beating our way out, so we compared notes briefly. During the recent unpleasantness, he had operated in occupied French Indochina. The Japanese exercised tighter control there than in Southeast China. I asked him how he got in.

"Jumped. At night. My Marconi would be dropped along with me on its own parachute. I would find a friendly village. Their houses were *bashas* with pitched roofs. I would get a small pole and smash the nodes out of a bamboo ridgepole so that I could string an antenna inside it. If no one had reported me to the Japanese by this time, I was reasonably secure for awhile.

"I would transmit at a different time each day and on a different frequency in accordance with a prearranged 'shedule.' I was restricted to exactly three minutes on the air no matter how much gen [British for Intelligence] I might have acquired.

"We had learned almost exactly how many days I could transmit before a Japanese direction finder would get a line on me. I could make one more transmission because they couldn't get a fix until a second

The last time I saw Southeast China. (Photos by Winborn)

Approaching Chihkiang Strip.

A Chinese C-47 finally showed up and Yamamura and I booked passage.

Good-bye to buddies at Changting Air Force Base, Weaver, Tucker, and Hacking.

direction finder picked me up. Then I would walk on to some other village.

"One night when I jumped in, the parachute on my Marconi flared and it was smashed to bits."

Stranded in the midst of occupied French Indochina without a Marconi! "That sounds like a bit of a predicament to find oneself in," I allowed. "What did you do next?"

"Aow, I walked to the nearest British hostel and sent a signal to the UK for another Marconi."

The day after we arrived in Chihkiang, we boarded an Air Force C-46 for Kunming. Ellis was gone when we got there. Peppler and I received navy orders to report to ComNavGrChina, Shanghai, so we caught another C-46 for Chihkiang. The next day we got on another for Shanghai. An hour or so out, it made a free-fall drop of some bundles on an American outpost. First it dragged the field and then came back, making the drop from an altitude of one hundred and twenty feet.

That afternoon we arrived over the great metropolis of Shanghai with its seven million people. The sprawling city and its tall buildings were a fantastic sight to those of us who had been out in the provinces for so long. After leaving Nanping we had traveled hard for two days by Jeep and had flown well over two thousand miles to reach another world—all of three hundred and seventy-five miles from Nanping.

The Chinese hadn't found time to regenerate a government. It would still be weeks before the Sikh policemen, brought from India by the British, were again patrolling the streets of Shanghai. These bearded giants, wearing turbans, were renowned for their ability to control the smallish Chinese.

When we arrived in town, eighty thousand armed Japanese were still there along with two or three hundred Americans. It was the Japanese who maintained law and order. There was no looting. They'd put layers of hay in the beds of their trucks and their soldiers would loll in it while patrolling the streets with rifles cradled in their arms.

Two of us would be walking down an avenue as a truckload of our former enemies approached. We eyed each other, thinking, "I could have killed you without compunction, you bastard, you!" We stared at them. They stared at us. And the truck rolled on.

Approaching Kiangwan aerodrome. To those of us who had spent many months in the boondocks, the great city of Shanghai was an inspiring sight. (Photo by Winborn)

Japanese troops patrolling the main street of Shanghai. (Photo by Mattmiller)

When we reported in, we found there was no billet for either of us. More than twenty years later I happened to read a book that told how the navy, right after the Japanese surrender and before the Chinese Government had time to regroup, sent teams into the major Chinese ports to survey all port facilities—wharves, rail lines, truck routes, cranes, godowns, communications, utilities, etc.—and also to take soundings around the wharves. The book said that for some reason or other the intended leader of the team designated for Tsingtao, a city on the Shantung Peninsula, had not shown up until it was no longer politic to make such surveys. Tsingtao didn't get surveyed. I now suspect that Peppler had been slated for duty on my team in Tsingtao. I should have been delighted to have him. It took me more than twenty years to find out why I had been sent to Shanghai.

We soon learned that any naval personnel in Shanghai, not having firm billets, were going to be impressed into the Shore Patrol. What an awful comedown for officers who had had TAI duty! We were indeed in peril. I said, "Peppler, we have got to do some snooping—fast." We immediately set out prowling around town with our ears open.

The *Conti di Verdi*, an Italian liner, had arrived in Shanghai at precisely the wrong moment—just as World War II broke out. The Chinese promptly interned it as enemy property. When Peppler and I explored the Shanghai waterfront, we noticed a large heap of twisted steel. We were to learn that it was superstructure blasted from the *Conti di Verdi* by the Fourteenth Air Force. Three times the Fourteenth reported that it had sunk this ship. Then the Japanese towed it to Japan and broke it up for scrap steel.

We ran into a man hanging around the area. We gradually found out that he had been the chief steward on the *Conti di Verdi*. We spoke no Italian and he spoke no Mandarin, so conversation was difficult. We took his picture standing by the heap of scrap steel. He had worked for the enemy and lived reasonably well all those years. Now they were gone and he had no income. We took him to a good restaurant and bought him a large dinner, which he deeply appreciated.

One day Peppler and I found an unoccupied factory in which there were several hundred nearly completed Kamikaze torpedo launches, all powered with taxicab engines. No taxis were left on the streets of Shanghai. Each launch would carry a monster war head in its bow. If the war had still been on when the Seventh Fleet steamed up the Whangpoo River, a swarm of wildly maneuvering suicide torpedo boats would have come out to attack. None of their personnel would have survived, but in my not entirely uneducated opinion, American casualties would have outnumbered Japanese many times over.

Peppler and I walked out Nanking Lu to a confectioner's shop in the British Settlement. (Of course Nanking Lu became Bubbling Well Road out there.) The shop served long-forgotten luxuries like chocolate sundaes. The booths were tiny, and perforce we sat quite close to the attractive, tall, blond young gentleman across the aisle. We assumed he was another American and introduced ourselves. He spoke excellent English, perhaps more Oxonian than American. He said, "I am a Soviet."

It turned out that he had been in China all those years as a neutral alien—in some governmental position. He had traveled extensively. One time he was on a long train rolling across flat country. Suddenly, machine gun bullets came crashing through the overhead. An American fighter

Chief Steward of the *Conti di Verdi*, posing with superstructure blasted off his ship by Fourteenth Air Force bombers. (Photo byWinborn)

Winborn, Chief Steward, and Peppler in front of a captured armored car. (Photo by unidentified passerby)

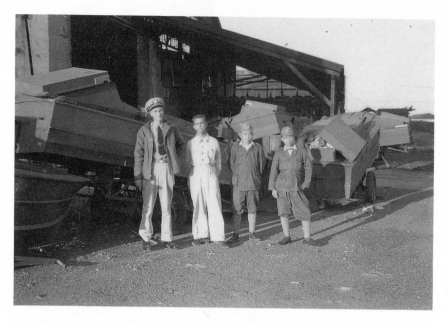

Japanese Kamikazi torpedo boats powered by confiscated taxicab engines, viewed by Peppler and the Chief Steward of the *Conti di Verde*. (Photo by Winborn)

was strafing the train. Casualties were in the hundreds. The locomotive blew up on the first pass. The fighter made a three-sixty, strafed the full length of the train again, and then broke off. More casualties. The Soviet was spared. I asked what the Chinese reaction to this attack by an American airplane had been. He said, "They cheered wildly—America was finally coming to China's assistance."

After the Bomb was dropped and everything was just about over, the Soviet's country declared war on Japan. Instead of being a neutral alien, he suddenly became an enemy alien. The Japanese caught up with him and threw him into jail. Just two hours later Japan surrendered and he was released.

In Shanghai, E. Phillips Oppenheim would have been considered to be a dull and unimaginative writer. If you wanted to hear a lively life story, you just stopped anyone on the street and started a conversation. I ran into one middle-aged woman who said that she was three-quarters Irish and one-quarter Cherokee Indian, and that she was an American citizen. She was born in San Francisco, kidnapped at some age between two and four, and taken to Siberia. The record of her birth was destroyed in the San Francisco fire. She had lived in Russia, the Philippines, and various places in China. One's first thought would be that she was probably a White Russian trying to wangle her way into the United States. But there was just a chance that her story was straight. She didn't ask for money.

13

SAVED BY

THE NAVAL AIR

PRIORITIES OFFICE

Peppler and I finally picked up some scuttlebutt that caught our undivided attention—it was rumored that a Lieutenant Commander Springer was trying to run a Naval Air Priorities Office with only one assistant, and that he was hopelessly swamped. Naval Air Priorities billets in turbulent Shanghai—now there was duty that could offer a real challenge to us! Everyone went out of his way to be cordial to a priorities officer—one never knew when he might want to fly. We looked up that commander, fast. He turned out to be a wonderful fellow except that he hadn't had duty out in Southeast China. I helped round up a bunch of renegade junior officers, most of whom had come in from the Chinese boondocks. The navy never had a more dedicated team for getting difficult missions accomplished, although at times our methods were a bit unorthodox.

Peppler received orders to sail from Shanghai on a slow ship so I didn't see him anymore. As for me, I put in for an extension of active duty to run the day-by-day operations at the air priorities office, while the skipper took care of the high level politics. When the Seventh Fleet steamed up the Whangpoo River, anchored just off the Bund, and took command of all naval forces in China, his duties became more vital than mine, believe me.

Ensign John Nolan Mattmiller was a good operator. We shared a room at the Park Hotel after Peppler got orders to return to the States.

Mattmiller was, of course, one of the NAPO team. During the war he had been stationed at a SACO unit which shadowed the port of Amoy. It was on Nine Dragons River, the only river in Southeast China in which it was safe to swim—no shistosomiasis. Mattmiller was a strong swimmer. At a swimming contest for Chinese soldiers, he picked out half a dozen prospects for special training. He had them practice by swimming against the current for prolonged periods. When his trainees got strong enough, Mattmiller had them swim with rocks tied to their chests. One soldier doing this got panicky and started floundering. The Chinese on the sampans all around could see clearly that river demons were after the hapless victim. They were all much too sage to try to thwart river demons. The soldier drowned.

When the rest of the soldiers were properly trained, Mattmiller got a junk and, during one dark night, they all sailed into the middle of the Amoy Harbor. As they neared a Japanese ship, they slipped over the side and swam out to it with limpet mines tied to their chests. Most of the mines were stuck along the side of the ship below the waterline. One was stuck near the propeller and rudder, and one was wrapped in a sock and tossed up on deck. The raiders swam back to their junk. They could see that a sailor was walking along the deck carrying a lantern. The mine on deck blew and the sailor with a lantern wasn't there any more. The other mines blew and the ship rolled over and sank in shallow water. After Amoy was evacuated, Mattmiller went out in the harbor and took pictures of his trophy.

The Cathay Hotel in downtown Shanghai was for lieutenant commanders and above. I was billeted there my first night in town and then was invited to move out to the Park Hotel, which was for junior officers. The Park was a fine building eighteen stories high and eleven years old. It was in the International Settlement right across Nanking Lu from the International Race Course. True, the Japanese had ripped the plumbing out of the Park and shipped it off to Japan as scrap steel. No problem—if an occupant wanted a little water for a bath or to flush a commode, all he had to do was call the desk and have them send up a houseboy with a bucketful. Mattmiller and I were very comfortable there.

Somehow Mattmiller got the two of us memberships in an exclusive

Japanese ship sunk by Mattmiller and his Chinese guerillas in shallow water, Amoy Harbor. (Photo by Mattmiller)

downtown luncheon club. The location was good, on the second floor. No sign or anything crass like that. Everything in good taste, but rather quiet and subdued, reflecting British influence, no doubt. The cuisine was excellent. The manager was a Turk. The membership included civilians from quite a few countries, but we were the only ones from the military. The club was a delightful spot for a little respite from the madhouse of our air priorities pursuit.

No beer and no imported liquor were available in the Shanghai stores. Our enlisted men's club was supplied all the good stateside beer that the men could possibly have wanted. The officers' club had only mixed drinks fabricated from local booze. The usual dosage was a sweetish pink concoction laced with vodka, which was distilled from fermented bread crumbs.

Two old Scotsmen still in Shanghai had run a Scotch whiskey business there before the War. They had imported prime whiskey from Scotland in barrels and bottled it in Shanghai. When the Japanese conquered the city, they confiscated the whiskey dealers' inventory and rationed it out to their officers at a rate calculated to last until the far-off end of the war. But the war was over before anyone thought it would be, leaving a sizable inventory on hand. The two dealers could have sold their stuff for—you name it—$100 gold a bottle? Yes, I think so, but they resolutely refused to sell to anybody but clients who planned to stay on in Shanghai and reestablish the prewar society.

Mattmiller just happened to become a friend of the old Scotsmen. They told him that what they really had a passion for was good, honest beer. Mattmiller cogitated, "Hm . . . beer . . . enlisted men's club . . . some really good pals there." He set up a predawn meeting. We drove there in a six-by-six and took aboard an impressive stock of fine stateside beer. Mattmiller took the beer over to his Scots friends and came back with a handsome supply of their whiskey. We gave a few bottles to our skipper, who used them to great advantage in entertaining some senior officers. Afterward he said, "The senior officers were amazed that such fine liquor could be served by a mere lieutenant commander."

The nightclubs and cabarets of Shanghai had dancing partners at so much per dance who might encourage you to buy drinks of questionable validity. If you wanted to take one of the women home, you could pay the management the amount that supposedly she would earn for them during the rest of the evening. The young women were not—repeat, *not*—prostitutes. Mostly they were refugees from drastic oppression in one part of the world or another, who found themselves in the exotic city of Shanghai with the necessity of supporting themselves.

One night about eleven, four of us "bought off" four attractive young women and set off into the night with them in my Jeep. They all lived in apartments in Honkew, on the other side of Soochow Creek, where about one hundred thousand Japanese lived. The area was strictly off-limits. As I dropped each woman off at her apartment, accompanied by one of my colleagues, I tried to remember where each one lived. Finally, there was just one girl left beside me.

I asked, "Who are you?"

She said, "Miriam."

I think that she was a German Jewess. She was pretty nice. So I kissed her warmly and took her to the entrance of her apartment. Then I back-tracked and somehow managed to pick up each of my three colleagues before driving back across the creek. Life in Shanghai surely wasn't dull.

During their long occupation of Shanghai, the Japanese had taken over the China Reserve Bank as a puppet organization and issued CRB notes as legal tender. When I arrived in town, CRB notes were still accepted, but it took $200 CRB to equal $1 CN and maybe $900 CN to equal $1 gold.[1] A rumor floated around Shanghai that one of the CRB notes had secret characters hidden in its engraving. After the notes were issued the Japanese noticed the characters. Of course they executed the engraver, but that didn't serve to impound the offending notes. I spent many hours scrutinizing CRB notes of all denominations and dates of issue. Finally on a 1944 $200 CRB note I found a concealed "A." Then I found an "S," a "U" and a "C." These characters stood for "United States Army Coming 1944." I soon became much too busy for this type of foolishness.

The Glen Line operated steamships in the Orient before the war. After the surrender, US Naval Group China took over the old Glen Line Building near the Bund. Did they post a sign saying "US Naval Group China"? Not this naval group. They put up a big sign saying, "United States Navy Pro Station."

The Naval Air Priorities Office occupied the fifth floor of the Glen Line Building. I was apt to be there any hour of the night or day. There was a small lobby on the ground floor in front of the elevators. One day a scraggly old amah[2] strode in and declared in a loud voice, "Me savvy Chinee writee. Me savvy English talkee. Wantum job."

"Personnel. Third floor."

Another time a rather slight, well-dressed and well-groomed young Chinese gentleman stepped into the lobby and said in a cultured voice, "In view of my superb advanced degree education and my exemplary innate competence, I suggest that I am eminently qualified for a position with the United States Navy Pro Station."

"Personnel. Third floor."

We suspected that his education might soon be broadened to the extent of learning what a prophylactic station was all about.

Quite a few affluent Chinese in Shanghai had stashed away their prewar automobiles in places the Japanese didn't find, and now they could let their cars see daylight again. There was no way they could get gas, oil, service, or particularly, parts. So a little custom sprang up— loan one's car to an American officer. Just perhaps, he might be able to do a little favor for you sometime. My skipper, who was tops, had acquired a prewar Plymouth in this fashion.

I was slated to work a predawn flight out at Lunghua. The skipper very kindly offered me the keys to his car. I fired it up in darkness and drove out to the aerodrome. The flight presented no problems. I had breakfast at the enlisted men's mess. The chow there was much superior to that at the officer's mess and the conversation was at least as good. Daylight returned while I was in the mess hall. After finishing breakfast, I found that my right front tire was flat.

The Fourteenth Air Force had moved into Lunghua. I was no longer attached to the outfit, but I still spoke the dialect. I located a likely-looking sergeant and said, "Sergeant, I have a flat tire on my Plymouth over there. Do you suppose you could have one of your men pull it off the rim and find out what's wrong with it?"

"Why, sure, Lieutenant."

Display at the entrance to the Enlisted Men's Mess, Lunghua Aerodrome (skull of an air raid victim). (Photo by Winborn)

I went around a corner to show the sergeant I knew he could handle his work without my watching him every minute. Pretty soon he came around and said, "That tire of yours has had it, Lieutenant. There is no way it can be repaired."

"Hm-m. We have a problem, don't we Sergeant. Do you have any good suggestions?"

"As a matter of fact, Lieutenant, I do." It seemed that a cargo ship loaded with military tires for the Fourteenth Air Force had recently made port. Topside had issued orders that all civilian tires on all Fourteenth Air Force surface vehicles must be replaced with proper military tires. The civilian tires had come from England, India, Japan, you name it. They were all thrown into a huge heap at one end of a hangar. A few of them were in good condition. The sergeant said that if he could find the right size, he would put one on my Plymouth.

After a while he came back and said, "Well, Lieutenant, you have got a tire." It looked practically new. I thanked him warmly and was all set to head back to town.

"How are your other three tires, Lieutenant?"

"You know, Sergeant, I haven't checked them lately." It would have been more exact to say that I had never seen them in daylight before.

Yes, they were all basket cases, and yes, the sergeant got me three more fine looking tires. I thanked him profusely and was about to leave when he asked, "How is your spare, Lieutenant?" The spare he found was almost as good as the other four.

I drove back to the office, gave the keys to the skipper, and said, "Thanks much."

A few hours later he looked me up and asked, "Winborn, where did you get those tires."

"Tires, Commander?"

"Yes, those new tires on my Plymouth."

"Oh, those tires," I said. "I have connections around this town."

I never did tell him how I got the tires. He was really a good guy, but he didn't have a need to know.

NAPO handled passengers for the Naval Air Transport Service which flew to Hawaii, Oakland and Washington, for a marine squadron which flew to Tientsin and Peiping, and for two patrol bomber squadrons which flew PBM flying boats north to Tsingtao and Jinsen (Korea) and south to Hong Kong and Manila. Our landplanes operated out of Kiangwan aerodrome north of town and our boats off the Whangpoo River at Lunghua to the south.

Sometimes we could get space for our overflow Washington passengers on the Army Air Transport Command's route back to Calcutta and on westward over India, the Middle East, Europe, and the Atlantic. We could accommodate accredited war correspondents (e.g. Claire Booth Luce), who had to pay the supposed commercial airline fare. We did not have a procedure for taking money from passengers, so we sent our revenue passengers over to the Air Transport Command, who did. We furnished the flight and they got the money. What the hell, we were all part of the same government and we worked together well at low levels like mine.

Life was hectic. As a typical example, we cleared a full load of passengers for a flight across the Pacific leaving at 2300 hours. The plane came in with a "mechanical" which would ground it for at least eight hours. We trucked the crew and the passengers back to Shanghai and they scattered in all directions. Less than an hour later, an unscheduled transport came in. No mechanicals, but the crew was way over hours. So my boys went to likely dives, found the original crew, who had not had time to get badly bent out of shape, pried them loose from their Russian girls, and poured coffee into them. Others of my gang rounded up all the passengers they could find, which was most of them. Then, with just a touch of embroidery, a couple of my boys strapped the pilots into their seats, pointed east and said, "Washington is that way, son," and got off that airplane fast before anyone could fire up those four big engines.

With all the running around involved, we obviously needed Jeeps, badly, but there were none in Shanghai. Captains and flag officers couldn't get them. We did have new deuce-and-a-half 6 x 6 trucks, and we loved them. Just about every day or so one of my boys would report that his six-by had had a slight altercation with a street car, which was now off the track. I'd ask my trusty stalwart to show me the six-by. No visible mark whatsoever, but six-bys simply were not appropriate for crooked, narrow streets clogged with rickshas, pedicabs, carts, bicycles, and civilians.

The horrors of warfare had swept beyond Okinawa months before, but some marines and seabees had been left there to wither on the vine. Life was duller than dishwater—until word spread around that Shanghai

Winborn and Mattmiller in front of a still armed PBM at Lunghua Aerodrome. The runway was made of Marston Matting, pierced steel sheet.
(Photo by unidentified passer-by)

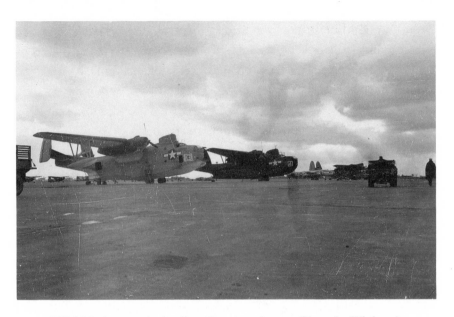

PBM Mariners parked at Lunghua Aerodrome. (Photo by Winborn)

An L-5 parked at Lunghua Aerodrome. (Photo by Mattmiller)

was one good liberty port—and only eight hundred miles away. The
marines and seabees would sweet-talk their way aboard any kind of
flight headed for Shanghai. One marine major cut himself orders to
"Proceed to Shanghai and familiarize yourself with conditions as they
now exist. Since no Government expense is warranted, none is
authorized." Then he signed the orders himself.

After a few days on the town, the fine young officers and gentlemen would go out to the aerodrome to sweet-talk their way aboard the
next flight to Okinawa. No way! The entire Shanghai zone was right
under the nose of Commander Seventh Fleet, and ComSeven had issued airtight orders applying to all naval personnel—"No priority, no
fly." So our allies from Okinawa would come traipsing back to the
Naval Air Priorities Office. But we, too, had strict orders from
ComSeven—"Boondoggling does not, repeat not, pull any kind of air
priority." If a boondoggler just had to get back to his base, he could
damn well go out to Topside's office aboard USS *St. Paul* and take his
reprimand.

We would tell our new friends, "You gentlemen have a problem.
You'll have to play ball with us very closely. Stay where we can reach
you at any moment and always be ready to go." Sure enough, pretty
soon an unscheduled flight would come in at 0200 and before daylight
we would have worked off some of our current inventory of
miscellaneous applicants for airplane rides, including, perhaps, certain
marines and seabees. Looking back on it, I don't know how we
accomplished this without making out one manifest for the pilot and a
somewhat abridged manifest to send out to the Seventh Fleet—no, we
didn't do that . . . .

Quite often one of our by now warm new friends would ask why
in the world we didn't use Jeeps. We would explain that there were no
Jeeps in Shanghai. Even senior officers couldn't get them. One of our
Okinawa seabee friends, a Lieutenant Richardson, said that he had so
many Jeeps on Okinawa that he was bulldozing them off the end of the
pier to make room for something else. He offered to give me all of them
I wanted. I said, "Thanks much, but those eight hundred miles of China

Sea do present a bit of a problem." He said, "That's your part of the problem—you're the one in the transportation business."

Our office would always be a madhouse while a manifest was being made up—sorting out who would get to fly and who wouldn't. Then, finally, one of our trucks would haul off all the winners and we would have a blissful interlude. During one of these lulls, I noticed a very young marine lieutenant standing at the counter. I went over and said, "Morning, Lieutenant. What can I do for you?"

"I—uh—I've got a C-46."

I allowed that that was a mighty nice thing to have.

"I am sick to death of island-hopping. Do you have any missions to the interior of China for me?"

Now NAPO didn't have a thing to do with dispatching airplanes. We just handled passengers for airplanes that somebody else dispatched. I saw no point in going into all that with the lieutenant. So I carefully shuffled through a stack of papers that happened to be on the counter. Finally, I said, "I'm sorry, Lieutenant, but I don't have a single mission to the interior today. But there is one thing you could do for me in the meantime. Just fly over to Okinawa, look up a Lieutenant Richardson of the seabees and bring back a couple of Jeeps he has for me. I'll surely keep you in mind the next time I do have something for the interior."

"Oh, all right."

Some of my boys met him when he landed at Kiangwan with the two Jeeps and sweet-talked him into making a second trip, which brought us two more. Those four Jeeps were perhaps a bit more war weary than Lieutenant Richardson had indicated, but my boys did a little cannibalizing and came up with three first-class Jeeps, complete with Okinawa registration numbers, which we were careful not to paint out.

Lieutenant Swentzel was in charge of the navy motor pool in Shanghai. My boys had no difficulty in establishing themselves as preferred customers for gasoline and parts. Not infrequently after that, one of them would be steaming down Nanking Lu at perhaps a mite above the regulation speed and an MP would flag him down. My boy would speed up and breeze on past. The MP would file a report on Jeep

Pigtails were a symbol of subservience when foreigners dominated Shanghai.
This is the only one that I observed. Photo taken in the French Concession.
(Photos by Winborn)

A residential street in the French Concession.

Street Scenes in the Old Chinese City

A place on Yates Road to buy "silks, satins, craps, and of all kinds piece goods."

Polylingual Shanghai

A school in Shanghai.

Pitched up eaves keep the demons out.

Vendor advertising his
wares—rat poison.

Lung Hwa Pagoda

Anyone walking down a street in Shanghai smoking a cigarette would be followed by a bunch of boys who engaged in a mad scramble for the butt when he discarded it. The boys would give the butts to a man whose vocation was to recover the unburned tobacco, roll it in new cigarette paper, and sell the reconstituted cigarettes.
Shown below.

Number. . . . Later on his superior would call him up and say, "You must have made an error, Corporal. No Jeep with that number is registered in Shanghai."

Captains and flag officers spotted our Jeeps soon enough. "What the blankety-blank are those junior officers doing riding around this town in Jeeps?"

Our skipper had his hands full with that one.

It was not long until some of the streets of Shanghai were crawling with Jeeps and officers' sedans. The bad guys in the streets soon learned how to hotwire them, so we routinely removed the distributor rotor whenever we parked one. The bad guys reacted by setting up a little factory to manufacture Jeep distributor rotors. All of us, good guys and bad guys alike, would go around with two or three rotors in our pockets. So my boys, with the help of a welder, rigged up a contraption with chain and padlock that could immobilize the gear shift lever and the steering wheel. When I shoved off from Shanghai, the bad guys hadn't as yet found out about bolt clippers.

A fairly large supply of prewar Chinese silver "dollars" circulated around Shanghai. As currency, it would take about nine hundred Chinese dollars to equal one dollar gold. But the Chinese dollars, beautiful coins, made prime souvenirs. They were worth about thirty-five cents for their silver content alone. Quite often on the street an urchin would grab your sleeve and say, "Hullo, Joe. Two Chinese dollars for one American dollar." Normally you would say, "*Chu-la, chu-la,*" meaning scram, but every once in a while it would be time to replenish your supply of Chinese dollars. If so, your answer would be, "No, no, no! Four Chinese dollars for one American dollar." This would start a big negotiation which would last about twenty minutes. A large crowd would gather around savoring the free show. Finally, one party or the other would give in and say, "Three Chinese dollars for one American dollar." The response would be "OK, OK," and the coins would exchange hands.

One time after all this rigmarole, the kid thrust the coins at me with his grubby little paws and immediately disappeared into the crowd. Wondering what kind of scam had been pulled on me, I inspected the three coins. The outer two were pre-War Chinese dollars in fine condition.

The inner one was a Spanish piece-of-eight dated 1798 in excellent shape. That smart kid had succeeded in palming off a coin he knew was not a good Chinese silver dollar.

Untold thousands of people in Shanghai rode to and from work on the streetcars. They were clerks, salespersons, people who were physically incapable of walking the long distances between their apartments and their places of work. If the streetcars were to stop running the workers would not be able to get to work, would not get paid, and would have to stop eating. So, when the streetcar crews announced that they were going to strike for higher wages, it appeared that Shanghai might be facing a disaster.

There was no disaster. During the strike, the streetcars ran as usual. Everybody got to work, got paid, and went on eating. One change was made in streetcar operating procedures—the conductors stopped collecting fares. The strike was settled promptly.

One day a French admiral showed me his orders at my counter in the Naval Air Priorities Office. They were very spongy. Whatever reason the admiral had for coming to Shanghai, it was not military. I was only too familiar with such orders. Strictly boondoggle. Priority zilch. And the Seventh Fleet had an edict—no priority, no free airplane ride courtesy of the US Navy. However, this admiral seemed to be a pretty decent sort and I happened to have one empty space that had just opened up. So I booked him to Washington.

It was hardly a minute before a US ensign showed up with red hot emergency leave orders. Class I priority. I booked him. Damn, I had an international incident on my hands. I was faced with bumping a French admiral to make room for an American ensign.

I sauntered over to where the admiral was standing along with everybody else waiting for the truck to the aerodrome. I struck up a conversation. "Had the Admiral enjoyed his stay in Shanghai?"

"Oh, it was all right."

"Did the Admiral have the baked Alaska at the Cathay?"

"Why, no. I didn't."

"Delicious. Had the Admiral enjoyed a dinner in the restaurant on top of the Wing On Department Store?"

"Why, no. That sounds interesting."

"Superb Chinese cuisine. Strictly immaculate, and a fine view of downtown Shanghai. Had the Admiral visited the Arcadia out on Avenue Joffre in the French Concession?"

"No, I fear not."

"Absolutely the best beef Stroganoff in the Orient. And the cutest little Chinese dancing girls. They sort of snuggle up to you when you dance with them."

The admiral almost reached a stage of incipient drooling.

"By any chance, would the Admiral care to extend his stay in Shanghai?"

"Yes, I believe that I should."

"I might be able to change your travel reservation for you, Admiral."

"Please do, if you can."

"Admiral, consider it done."

Next problem.

Another day, I got a predawn flight off from Lunghua without any difficulty and was driving back to Shanghai in my Jeep. While still out in the country, I came across an American JG on foot, probably beating his way back after a heavy date with a Russian girl. By the time we reached the middle of town, we had become old buddies. He invited me to have breakfast aboard the LST which he commanded, now moored out in the Whangpoo River.

After we had finished chow, we sat around the wardroom swapping sea stories, as naval officers sometimes do. Among other things, he told about an incident which had occurred during their cruise while the war was still on. His LST was in convoy under strict orders to observe radio silence. They were at sea far away from any base when one of the men came down with severe abdominal pains. No medical officer was aboard, but a pharmacist's mate thought that the symptoms might indicate appendicitis. The patient's condition worsened. Finally the skipper decided that he just had to break radio silence and call for a PBY flying boat (Dumbo) to come out and transport the man to a base hospital.

Dumbo appeared over the horizon, and its pilot, with great skill, landed safely in a heavy seaway. The LST dropped out of convoy, which was a dangerous thing to do, and launched a small boat which carried the patient over to the PBY, now wallowing in the waves, and then stood off. The pilot waited for the sea to come up with a relatively level patch and then gunned his engines. He had accelerated his flying machine almost up to liftoff speed when a massive wave welled up and slapped the right wing off the airplane.

The small boat retrieved all hands. The PBY refused to sink, but kept bobbing around in the angry waves. This would never do because the Japanese might recover it, gaining a package of valuable intelligence. So the LST had to break out its deck gun and lob rounds into the wreck until it sank.

The next day another PBY flew over and circled around and around looking for its sister ship which hadn't come home. Finally my friend reluctantly broke radio silence again and called, "Return to base. Your PBY has sunk. All hands are safe aboard this LST."

He summed up his story by saying, "So we had to drop out of convoy, which was hazardous, break radio silence twice, which was against all orders, and cause the loss of an airplane, which would be sorely missed."

As had been expected, I piped up and asked, "And what happened to the appendicitis case?

"Oh, three days later we sailed into Majuro and rushed him to a medical officer. Doc queried him about his personal habits and found that they had been highly irregular. So he gave the sailor a strong physic and pretty soon the man felt just fine again."

The October 1945 Ten Ten Day[3] celebration in Shanghai was particularly ebullient because victory could finally be proclaimed in the long, grinding war against Japan. Parades rolled out Nanking Lu. Huge crowds seemed to be everywhere. We all celebrated.

A couple of friends dropped around to our room in the Park Hotel in the middle of an evening. It appeared that it might be a good time for a very minor party. One of us went out and bought a bottle of vodka just before the store closed. When the bottle was unwrapped, it was noticed that a sizable bug was swirling around at the bottom. The idea of having

Ten Ten Day in Shanghai

People everywhere.

The Generalissimo on Ten Ten Day.

Floral tramcars pass under the victory arch.

The captured Japanese plane almost flew in the window of the Park Hotel. On the ground is the International Race Course.

From the Park Hotel a view of V for Victory on Ten Ten Day.

a party almost collapsed. Then one of us sagely observed, "It would be possible to draw a little bit of vodka off the top of the bottle without getting anywhere near the bug."

You know the rest of this story. A while later that bug was high and dry at the bottom of an empty bottle.

I had heard from a not very reliable source that the "Flag" was aboard USS *St. Paul* out there in the Whangpoo River. That meant to me that ComSeven had his offices aboard that ship and that everything about it must be cold-four-O-perfection. I was delighted when one of her officers invited me to have dinner aboard his ship. Some real American chow at last!

Somehow the chow didn't seem to be all that wonderful. The freshly baked bread was good, for instance, but it had little dark flecks all through it. It turned out that the ship's flour had gone weevilly. The commissary officer had taken a specimen to the medical officer. The medical officer had determined that any—ah—unfortunate connotations of weevildom would be taken care of by the baking process, and all that would remain would be tiny bits of digestible protein. The ship's diet at the time was perhaps a mite low on protein, and besides there was no possibility of getting a new supply of wheat flour in Shanghai. So the present store was approved for normal consumption.[4]

You know, I was quite happy to get back on the beach and resume subsistence on familiar Chinese cooking.

One day during the madhouse of making up the manifest for the next flight, a young enlisted man came up to the counter. His orders to report for duty aboard his ship were quite proper. The only problem was that he hadn't been able to catch his ship—for thirteen months. Each time he got to the port where it was supposed to be, he found that it had just sailed. He had his financial voucher with him, so he could draw his pay from any Navy Disbursing Officer. He sent letters home, but in all that time he had received no mail.

I called the Captain of the Port. Yes, his ship had just sailed. The Captain told me where it was headed. I could not pass this information on to the man because it was classified. I gave him a priority to our stop nearest to where his ship was headed and wished him luck.

USS *Nashville* anchored in the Whangpoo across from the Bund.

Whangpoo River at the Bund.

Running a Naval Air Priorities office in downtown Shanghai, keeping in close touch with operations at outlying aerodromes, and supposedly clearing everything with ComSeven generated a massive requirement for reliable electrical communications.

Before the war, Shanghai had had a good telephone system operated by IT&T. But years of occupation had left it in a shambles. To call operations at Kiangwan, we couldn't just give a number to the operator. No, we had to select another exchange and ask the local operator to connect us. Then we would ask the operator of that exchange to connect us with still another exchange, working our way out toward Kiangwan. When we got most of the way there, we would often find ourselves in a cul-de-sac. Unplug all connections and start over again on a different route. It was possible that we might eventually get through.

Our skipper induced some Signal Corps personnel to string a wire all the way out to Kiangwan Operations. At each end we had an army field telephone instrument in its leather case with a magneto that could be cranked to ring the bell at the other end; but copper wire was very precious and thieves gave a high priority to pilfering it. Then our skipper got us a good radio transceiver with an antenna on the roof. At first this antenna was a pilferable item, but pretty soon ComNavGrChina tightened up on the security in its building.

One day I could transmit to Kiangwan on the field telephone but couldn't receive. I could receive on the radio but couldn't transmit. Communication was possible, but hardly on a plane befitting the dignity of a modern around the world airline.

Our radio finally became fully operational. One time I worked far into the night and was still there at daybreak. (Flights were as likely to take off at 0300 as 1500.) My radio receiver was still on because I hadn't turned it off. A marine outfit in northern China came on the air and tried to work ComSeven. No radioman in the entire Seventh Fleet was monitoring the command frequency. I broke in and called the marine outfit. I introduced myself and offered to relay its message to ComSeven when somebody out there finally woke up. The marines were most grateful.

Their message was a priority operational dispatch. A marine aircraft had made a forced landing in northern China. Communists had taken the crew prisoner, and confiscated the aircraft. The marines considered this to be a major international incident. They were deeply concerned over the fate of the crew, and urgently requested instructions from ComSeven as to what actions to take. Perhaps two hours elapsed before anyone in ComSeven answered my repeated calls and gave me a roger on the marines' message. I went back to the Park Hotel to take a delayed nap.

Many details of the incident were written up in the stateside newspapers. But to my knowledge this is the first time that the detail of NAPO's role in the affair has been committed to paper. The Communists eventually released the prisoners. The aircraft was never returned.

The big white navy hospital ship was moored near one end of the Bund. I just happened to become acquainted with a young nurse who had come ashore. I took her out to dinner at the truly excellent restaurant on top of the Wing On Department Store and ordered a superb Chinese dinner with birds' nests in sweet almond cream for dessert. It was all so foreign to her that she couldn't touch a thing. I had to take her back to her ship so that she could get a sandwich before the galley closed for the night. Come to think of it, I never saw that nurse again.

The American Armed Forces in Shanghai decided, weeks in advance, to stage a giant all-China Army-Navy football classic. The date was set for 1 December 1945, the same date as the annual Army-Navy football game in the States. The place was the Velodrome in Shanghai.

The navy quietly made a survey of all its personnel in the Asiatic-Pacific Theater and located a goodly number of outstanding football stars, ordering them to report for temporary additional duty in Shanghai. The army found out about this a week before the great event and was furious. It insisted that no more football stars should be ordered to Shanghai. The navy acquiesced, maybe because this assured that no army stars could be brought in at the last moment.

Only U.S. Armed Forces and UNRRA personnel were admitted to

the game, some ten thousand of them. The contest was so lopsided that it was pathetic to watch. Most of us didn't stay for the finish.

A great ricksha derby, starting at the navy pier and ending at the Velodrome, was held immediately prior to the football game. Nineteen rickshas were entered, sponsored by various American military offices around town. The "jockeys" were girls who worked in these offices, two of them American and the rest assorted Shanghai types. The winner was to be proclaimed "Miss Ricksha of 1945." The ricksha coolies were carefully selected from those who made this their career. They had been placed under controlled diets on training tables and conditioned by having them lope for many kilometers behind Jeeps, with speeds and distances gradually increasing as they became stronger athletes. The winning coolie was to be honored by having a wreath of flowers placed around his neck. A cash award of $7,000,000 CRB was also promised, which converted to less than $40 gold. I never heard how this was to be divided between the winning jockey and the coolie, or if the cash prize was actually awarded. Maybe this award was something greater than the sponsors could raise.

My outfit, NAPO, was much too busy to engage in such foolishness. Besides, we had no girls in our hectic office.

---

[1] I still have a 50-cent CRB note. Hopefully it is now worth more as a curio than as legal tender.

[2] A female servant.

[3] On October 10, 1911, an accidental uprising in Wuchang on the Yangtze River had finally touched off a long simmering revolution, resulting in the collapse of the last of the dynasties whose emperors had ruled China for more than three millenia. China became a republic; its first president was Sun Yat Sen. Thereafter, the Chinese Nationalist party had treated Ten Ten Day as the leading national holiday.

[4] I learned many years later, ComSeven's flag really flew from USS *Mount Olympus* at the time.

Army–Navy Game, 1 December 1945, Velodrome, Shanghai

Derby Day winning jockey, June Negaard, with
Lieutenant General Stratemeyer

Front page of *The Stars and Stripes*, China Bowl Supplement,
announcing the Derby Day jockeys, and in the box the "owners."

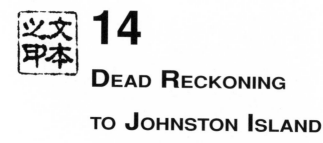

14

DEAD RECKONING

TO JOHNSTON ISLAND

A few years ago my fine nephew Dan Travis asked, "Have you ever navigated by dead reckoning?" This is computation of a ship's (or aircraft's) position some time after proceeding from a known location done without astronomical or electronic inputs. I replied, "Yes, Dan, I have." And recounted the story of my flight back to American territory.

December was slipping past and I was still in Shanghai. I had to admit that our airlines business had tapered off a lot. I had already received a dispatch reading "PROCEED TO ANACOSTIA FOR REASSIGNMENT." But "proceed for reassignment" orders didn't pull any kind of an air priority and I certainly didn't relish the idea of spending months aboard some crummy, jam-packed surface vessel after coming more than halfway around the world by air. Besides, I still enjoyed life in Shanghai, even though things were closing in on me a bit.

I happened to run into Lieutenant Commander Smith, skipper of patrol bomber squadron VPB-17. My team and I had frequently toted him and his people around town in our Jeeps. He said that his squadron was being relieved and that he was to fly his particular war weary PBM back to Kaneohe Bay on Oahu where it would be turned in for survey. I was delighted when he asked, "Would you like to be a passenger on the flight as my guest?"

We lifted off the Whangpoo on the twenty-first and landed in Chimu Wan, a bay in Okinawa, spending the night aboard a seaplane tender. The next day we flew on to Saipan. A small but persistent oil leak had

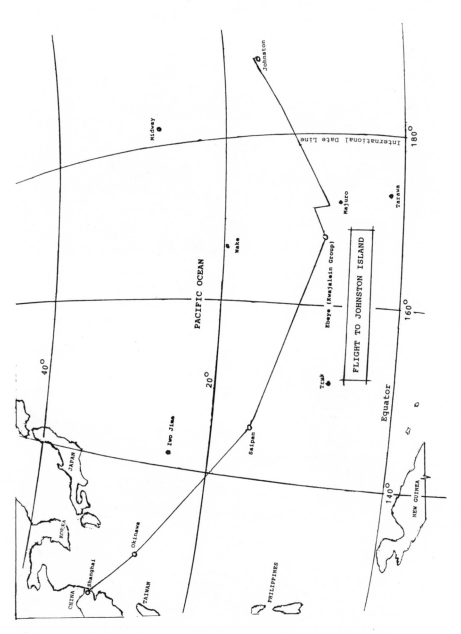

(Map by Byron Winborn)

PBMs on the Whangpoo River, near Lunghua Aerodrome, Shanghai. Above, US
Navy vessel moored down-river from the PBM. (Photos by Winborn)

developed behind the port engine. The skipper, known as the Patrol Plane Commander aboard a PBM, had the old boat hauled up on the ramp for inspection. The mechanics found that the leak was buried deep in the spinach aft of the big R-2800 engine, which would have to be pulled to correct the problem. This would take days, so the PPC, who in this case was also Squadron Commander, had the boat put back into the lagoon. The next day we cruised on over to Ebeye Island in the Kwajalein Group.

As we were coming in to Ebeye we noticed a sister PBM piled high up on the reef around the lagoon. It seems that a strong blow had come up during the night and the rusted mooring had parted. One of the men standing watch aboard the boat began trying to get the auxiliary engine running—"Pup-pup-pup-pup." The auxiliary engine, if it ever started, would drive a generator which could put out enough power to start the two big engines. The men on watch could then taxi into the wind and keep their boat off the reef until the wind let down and a small boat could come out and tow them in. The other man on the watch got on the radio using battery power. "Ebeye Tower, this is Box 8. Mayday— Mayday—Mayday. We have parted our mooring and are drifting toward the reef." "Pup-pup-pup-pup." Profanity. "Pup-pup-pup-pup." "Ebeye Tower, this is Box 8. Mayday—Mayday—Mayday—"

After quite a long spell, a strong, calm signal came on the air, "Box 8, this is Ebeye Tower. I read you five by five. How do you read me? Over."

C-R-A-S-H!

The PBM was the world's heaviest operational two engine airplane. A high wing monoplane, it had two decks forward with a galley below and the flight deck above. It had a forward bunkroom and an after bunkroom for use on long flights. A torpedo bay that could accommodate a full-sized aerial torpedo or an array of bombs was located aft of each engine. A large compartment in the after-portion of the fuselage would carry passengers and cargo. We were particularly heavy on this journey because, in addition to an oversized crew, part of whom usually stayed on the beach, we carried a black-shoe captain, a black-shoe lieutenant on emergency leave, and me.[1] Everybody aboard was leaving China for the last time and we all carried more gear than usual.

The next leg of our journey was to be to Johnston Island, a mere speck of land fourteen hundred and forty nautical miles away, so we were going to carry full tanks. The PPC, a terrific officer, decided to delay takeoff until dusk so that we would have daylight to help us find Johnston the next morning. If we couldn't find it, at least we would have daylight for an open sea landing and better prospects of being spotted by a rescue plane. The PPC hadn't planned it that way, but the delayed takeoff gave everybody an opportunity for some heavy partying the night before.

It seemed that we must have taxied halfway across the Pacific before we finally "unstuck," as the Limeys say. As soon as we were airborne it was night, which comes on so rapidly in the tropics. It became apparent that the navigator had not recovered at all from his binge the night before. The copilot was sharp at getting good celestial shots on the bubble sextant, but he couldn't hack the arithmetic involved in feeding the sextant data into the Air Almanac and getting a line of position out. I didn't have the know-how required to take a shot, but I was quite handy at a bit of arithmetic. The copilot and I were jointly designated navigator. For our first fix, our three lines of position crossed in a neat little triangle. We proudly showed it to the old black-shoe captain. He snorted, "If you can't put your foot through a fix, something is wrong with it. Yours is no damn good." From then on we pretty much got fixes that you could put your foot through.

Two hours into the night, someone noticed black engine oil dripping down into the doorway in the bulkhead between the two bunkrooms. Some of the crew broke out the Aldis lamp and, sure enough, a sizeable stream of oil was trailing out into the night from the aft end of the port torpedo bay. Perhaps our small leak had grown up to become a big one. At this rate the port engine would never survive until daybreak, and we were much too heavy to stay in the air on one engine.

The PPC asked us joint navigators which American base was nearest. We said Majuro. He asked us for a course from present position to Majuro. We ran it off, more than a ninety-degree change, and he headed onto the new course immediately. He put the radioman on the air trying to raise Majuro to request clearance for an emergency night landing.

To make ready for an emergency night landing was a prodigious task. Majuro would have to break out its small boats and then anchor flares at close intervals along both sides of what would become a seaway in their lagoon. The seaway would be at least a mile long and would have to be aligned with the wind. To make matters worse, it was Christmas Eve and Majuro was running low on liquor for its party. All its radio facilities were engaged in working nearby islands trying to find somebody who could alleviate the situation. They were much too busy to handle our request for an emergency night landing.

As all of this was going on, the plane captain felt awful. He was a conscientious kid and the officers and crew all thought a lot of him. He hadn't considered himself good enough for the billet, but the skipper had told him that he was, and he had taken over well. Now he was the one who had been responsible for preparing the airplane for this flight. He had delegated the task of filling the oil tank for the port engine to one of the other crewmen. He now requested, and was granted, permission to open a hatch in the overhead and crawl out inside the big wing to the torpedo bay aft of the port engine. A small man could do this provided, of course, that he was not wearing a parachute. The plane captain crawled out there with a flashlight. He came back and reported that the cap had not been properly secured on the filler neck of the port oil tank, but was now dangling on its little piece of chain. That was where the oil was escaping. This made us feel somewhat better because, maybe, when the oil got low enough the spillage would slack off. Maybe.

The plane captain still felt awful. He again requested, and was granted, permission to crawl out into the wing. This time when he came back he reported that he had stood on the doors at the bottom of the torpedo bay and had just barely been able to reach up with both hands and get the cap back on. Some of the crew broke out the Aldis lamp and found that the flow of oil out into the night had ceased.

Our plane didn't have oil quantity gauges, and the oil pressure gauges on the instrument panel would show nothing amiss until the oil was gone. The PPC asked us navigators to give him a new course from present position to Johnston. He turned onto it as soon as we gave it to him.

The plane captain talked to one of the squadron officers, saying, "You know, Mr. Black, the doors at the bottoms of the torpedo bays are spring-loaded to open at a weight of one hundred and fifty pounds so that if a bomb carries away from its shackle, it will be dropped into the sea instead of being brought home where it might blow up on landing. I weigh one hundred and forty-five pounds, and I was really praying when I stood on those doors."

Some time later the radioman got on the intercom and said, "Mr. Smith, I finally got an acknowledgment from Majuro on our emergency night landing request."

"Ah-h," said the PPC, "I guess that in all the excitement back there we forgot to tell you—the oil leak has been corrected and we have resumed course to Johnston."

"Aye, Sir. Do you want me to cancel our emergency night landing request?"

"Ah-h, wait twenty minutes and then cancel it."

We had crossed the International Date Line, so it was 24 December for the second day in a row. After a few more hours daylight returned and that ended celestial navigation. We had loran, but all that it showed was an unintelligible mess of weeds. Our radar could reach out only twenty-eight miles. We had known before we started that the Johnston radio range was inoperative, but we could read our indicated airspeed and our altitude so we could calculate true airspeed. We could estimate wind speed and direction by observing a driftmeter set into the deck. We had a gyrofluxgate compass that was corrected for deviation. Magnetic variation for the area was given on our charts. We had a chronometer. We could calculate position points and we kept plotting them on the chart. The plot indicated that we were approaching Johnston, but we couldn't see anything except ocean. Finally, our latest point fell right on Johnston. Nothing was in sight except beautiful blue Pacific— no land, no ship, no other airplane. It is hard to imagine so much empty ocean.

The PPC had our radioman call Johnston. He raised them easily. Johnston had our radioman send out MOs. In Morse Code, MO is "— —." A continuous series of MOs is the accepted signal to be used when a radio-direction-finding bearing is needed. Johnston gave us the bearing, which called for a ninety degree increase in course (turn south, if you are headed east). In just minutes, our radar started bringing in Johnston. When our position point on the chart had showed us right over the island, we had been exactly thirty-five nautical miles due north of it.

We came in on our approach and landed with the usual jolt of hitting water at seventy-five knots. The epic flight was over. The port engine had survived; so had all of us. When we got ashore we could see how bedraggled our PBM looked with the side of its fuselage all fouled up with black engine oil. But that was all right—that old PBM had carried us safely back to American territory.

---

[1] In the navy, a black-shoe officer was one qualified for sea duty or underseas duty, as contrasted to a brown-shoe officer who was in the naval air organization. I wore brown shoes when I was in uniform.

Box 2 at Ebeye Island.

Airplanes lined up at Ebeye Island.

Every atoll had to have one of these.

Patrol Plane
Commander Smith
flying his PBM over
the Pacific.

Passenger Winborn
flying the PBM over
the Pacific just as
though he knew how.

PBM in flight
looking forward
from the dorsal gun
mount.

PBM in flight looking aft from the dorsal gun turret toward the horizontal tail.

Patrol Plane Commander Red Smith at Johnston Island with his PBM all fouled up with engine oil.

Epilogue

The victorious Kuomintang was driven out of mainland China by the Communists in 1949 and it set up an independent nation on the island of Taiwan. During the 1960s, after I had retired from the Naval Reserve and was employed in the defense industry, I was making a business trip in a Convair 340. The gentleman seated across the aisle from me was Chinese. We struck up a conversation.

My fellow passenger turned out to be the Minister of Education for the Republic of China, Taiwan. He was making a tour of selected cities in the United States to learn what he could about the educational systems. This task was nearly completed, and he said, regretfully, it had not been productive because the educational system in Taiwan was already far superior to anything in the States.

During our conversation, I drew upon some of my knowledge of the Chinese language. The airplane landed, and as we parted we shook hands and he told me, "You have learned an amazing amount of our language considering the very brief time you spent in our country. But you speak with a terrible peasant accent."

The Winborn Boys: from left to right, Byron, Jim and Dade. Jim (James Henderson Winborn), married with small children, received a commission as a supply officer in the US Naval Reserve shortly after this picture was taken. He was stationed at Naval Operating Base, Norfolk. He died suddenly in 1960. Dade (Morris Knight Winborn), received a commission in the US Naval Reserve before Pearl Harbor and served as a deck officer on the US *Platte*, an oiler—hazardous duty. Later in the war he became a blimp pilot—good duty. He became a Lt. Commander before Byron did. He now lives in San Diego.

Advertisments that ran in 1994 in two Hong Kong papers in the search for Willie Ho.

GLOSSARY

a–bag—a strong canvas bag with four flaps at one end secured by a snap on the carrying strap

ack-ack—anti-aircraft fire

AGAS—Air-Ground Aid Service; reported to White House

AGFRTS—Air-Ground Forces Resources Technical Staff; Fourteenth Air Force, associated with OSS

ATC—Air Transport Command, Army Air Force

AUS—the body of personnel on active service in the United States Army composed of temporarily promoted officers, draftees, members of the Army Reserve and National Guard, etc.

AVG—American Volunteer Group

B-24—US Army Air Force "Liberator" heavy bomber made by Consolidated with four P&WA* R-1830 engines

B-25—US Army Air Force "Mitchell" medium bomber made by North American with two Wright R-2600 engines

B-29—US Army Air Force "Super Fortress" heavy bomber made by Boeing with four Wright R-3350 engines

bazooka—long, open-ended, tubular weapon which fired an explosive rocket

bei kan jiu—a raw white brandy made from rice

black shoe—member of the surface or underseas navy, whose uniform regulations stipulated black shoes, as contrasted to members of the Naval Air Organization whose uniforms also included aviation green with brown shoes

BMM—British Military Mission, Pucheng

"buffalo milk"—ice cream; actually ice cream made from TAI's dwindling supply of mix brought to Southeast China before the Corridor was captured

BuPers—Bureau of Personnel, Navy Department

C-46—US Army Air Force "Commando" transport made by Curtiss-Wright with two P&WA* R-2800 engines

C-47—US Army Air Force "Skytrain" transport made by Douglas with two P&WA* R-1830 engines. The Air Force version of the commercial DC-3

C-54—US Army Air Force "Skymaster" transport made by Douglas with four P&WA* R-2000 engines. The Air Force version of the commercial DC-4

CAMM—Chief Aviation Machinist Mate, a navy petty officer rating

CSK—Chief storekeeper, a navy petty officer rating

catty—the English word for a unit of weight used in Eastern Asia; a catty was equivalent to about one and one-third pounds avoirdupois

chop—an individual's official stamp or seal used in lieu of a signature in China

chu-la, chu-la—"chu" means "go," "la" makes the word sound better but does not add meaning; a way to say "scram"

CNAC—China National Aviation Corporation; a PanAmerican affiliate

commissioner—a higher-up civilian official

ComNavGrChina—Commander, Naval Group China; called ComNavFor China for a while in 1945

ComSeven—Commander Seventh Fleet, US Navy

Convair 340—Forty-four passenger commercial transport made by Consolidated-Vultee with two P&WA* R-2800 engines

cormorant—a bird used for catching fish; rings were placed around the cormorant's neck to prevent it from swallowing any fish caught

corridor—strip of land conquered by the Japanese in 1944 that encompassed the railway line running from the triple cities on the Yangtze River down to the Southeast China coast around Quangchow

DC-3—Twenty-one to twenty-eight passenger commercial transport made by Douglas with two P&WA* R-1830 engines

DC-4—fifty-two passenger (typically) commercial transport made by Douglas with four P&WA* R-2000 engines

Dakota—Royal Air Force version of the C-47 Transport

Deuce-and-a-half—see six-by-six

.45 Automatic—US Pistol, caliber 0.45, Model of 1911, Colt semiautomatic; more acclaimed for its stopping power than for its accuracy

14th AF—Fourteenth Air Force; headquarters Kunming

Frank—Japanese Army single-seat fighter made by Nakajima with one Nakajima Model Ha45 eighteen-cylinder radial air-cooled engine

FW-190—Designation commonly used in US for German Focke-Wulf Fw 190 single-seat fighter with 1 BMW D2 2100 Hp radial air-cooled engine

French Indochina—1945 terminology for the states of Cambodia, Laos, North Vietnam and South Vietnam

hao, hao, hao—literally "good, good, good" but used as an affirmative, which is lacking in Chinese

HQ—3rd War Zone—Wutu

HQ 13th AF—Kienow

hua-la, hua-la—"talk, talk," "*la*" makes it sound better

Hump Run—air route over the Himalayas between Assam in northern India and Southwest China, principally Kunming

JRB—US Navy light transport made by Beech with two Wright R-7760 engines

Jeep—US Army 1/4 ton GPW (whence "Jeep") truck, 4 x 4 (four wheels, all driving)

jing bao—air raid alarm; always used by the Americans as well as the Chinese

kan bei—"bottoms up"; literally, "dry glass"

kiang—river

leng kai shui—"cooled boiled water"

li—unit of distance used for walking or travel by sampan; a somewhat flexible term, about one-third of a mile or one-half a kilometer

LST—Landing Ship Tank

lu—road

magistrate—civilian official; a term used very loosely by Americans

Mayday—international radio distress call

MCAS—Marine Corps Air Station

ME-109—Designation commonly used in US for German Messerschmitt Bf 109 single-seat fighter with one DB605D 1800 Hp liquid-cooled inverted V engine

mei kuo ren—literally "beautiful country person"; the Chinese expression for American

M1 Carbine—light, short-barreled, gas-operated, magazine fed 0.30 caliber rifle weighing about five pounds; carbines were originally devised for cavalry on horseback

M1 Rifle—semi-automatic, gas-operated 0.30 caliber rifle; standard army rifle for WWII

M1903 Rifle—magazine fed bolt action 0.30 cal. rifle developed by Springfield Armory; standard rifle during WWI, preferred by some during WWII

MO—in Morse code, MO is — —; MO is the signal used for radio-direction-finding

NAPO—Naval Air Priority Office (Shanghai)

NAS—Naval Air Station

Nate—Japanese Army Type 87 single-seat fighter with one Nakajima Type 97 650 Hp. nine cylinder radial air-cooled engine

NATS—Naval Air Transport Service

OK—for all intents and purposes, the Chinese assimilated the American expression "OK"

OCH—Old China Hand; meaning someone who had been in China for a while and knew his way around.

OSS—Office of Strategic Services; Colonel "Wild Bill" Donovan's predecessor to CIA

OWI—Office of War Information; civilian

P-38—US Army Air Force "Lightning" single-seat fighter made by Lockheed with two twelve-cylinder Allison V-1710 liquid-cooled engines

P-40—US Army Air Force "Tomahawk" and later "Warhawk" single-seat fighter made by Curtiss-Wright with one twelve-cylinder Allison V-1710 liquid-cooled engine

P-51—US Army Air Force "Mustang" single-seat fighter made by North American with one Packard-built twelve-cylinder Rolls-Royce V-1650 engine

PBM—US Navy "Mariner" patrol bomber flying boat made by Martin with two P&WA* R-2800 engines (early models had two Wright R-2600 engines)

PBY—US Navy "Catalina" patrol bomber flying boat made by Consolidated with two P&WA* R-1830 engines

Peiping—1945 name for the city now (and previously) called "Beijing"

PPC—Patrol Plane Commander (navy)

Quangchow—Chinese name for Canton

R4-D—US Navy transport made by Douglas. Navy version of the commercial DC-3

R5-D—US Navy transport made by Douglas. Navy version of the commercial DC-4

Retread—military officer or enlisted man who was retired and subsequently recalled to active duty

SACO—Sino-American Cooperative Organization; US Navy

Sally—Japanese Army Type 97 heavy bomber made by Mitsubishi with two Mitsubishi fourteen cylinder radial air-cooled engines

Seaplane Tender—a naval vessel used to support seaplane operations

Six-by-six (also six-by, 6 x 6)—Army 2 1/2 ton truck with two front wheels and four rear wheels, all driving

SNJ—US Navy two-seat advanced trainer made by North American with one P&WA* R-1350 engine

sui bien—decline tactfully

Superior private—Chinese rating equivalent to US private first class

survey—a US Navy term for "scrapping out"

ta tien hua—telephone

TAI—Technical Air Intelligence; Army-Navy-British

Taiwan—Chinese name for Formosa

30-06 Ammunition—0.30 caliber rifle round approved by the Army in 1906

.38 Revolver—Smith and Wesson 0.38 caliber revolver; more accurate than the 0.45 automatic

triple cities—Hankow, Hanyang and Wuhan, adjoining cities on the Yangtze River

Tony—Japanese Army Type 3 Kawasaki Fighter with one Kawasaki Model Hp 140 twelve cylinder liquid-cooled inverted-V engine

tu fei—bandit

12.7 mm gun—Japanese machine gun comparable to the American .50 caliber machine gun

20 mm cannon—automatic, firing 20 mm incendiary, armor piercing, anti-personnel and tracer explosive projectiles

USA—United States Army (regular)

USN—United States Navy (regular)

USNR—United States Naval Reserve

VPB 17—US Navy Patrol Bomber Squadron No. 17

VPB 20—US Navy Patrol Bomber Squadron No. 20

WASC—War Area Service Command; hostels in various locations

Weapons Carrier—a 4 x 4 utility vehicle, typically carrying eight passengers and miscellaneous material

ying—British

Zeke—Japanese Navy Type O fighter made by Nakajima and Mitsubishi with one Nakajima fourteen cylinder radial air-cooled engine. Commonly called the "Zero" in the United States

---

*P&WA indicates Pratt & Whitney Aircraft, a leading engine company

INDEX